HERBLOCK
ON ALL
FRONTS

HERBLOCK ON ALL FRONTS

TEXT AND CARTOONS BY
HERBERT BLOCK

NEW AMERICAN LIBRARY

TIMES MIRROR

NAL BOOKS TRADEMARK REG. U.S. PAT. OFF. AND FOREIGN COUNTRIES
REGISTERED TRADEMARK—MARCA REGISTRADA
HECHO EN CRAWFORDSVILLE, INDIANA, U.S.A.

SIGNET, SIGNET CLASSICS, MENTOR, PLUME,
MERIDIAN and NAL BOOKS are published by
The New American Library, Inc.,
1633 Broadway, New York, New York 10019

Library of Congress Cataloging in Publication Data

Block, Herbert, 1909-
Herblock on all fronts.

1. United States—Politics and government—1977-
—Caricatures and cartoons. 2. United States—
Politics and government—1969-1974—Caricatures and
cartoons. 3. United States—Politics and government
—1974-1977—Caricatures and cartoons.
4. United States—Social conditions—1960-
—Caricatures and cartoons. 5. American wit and
humor, Pictorial. I. Title.
E872.B57   320.973'0207   80-18182
ISBN 0-453-00389-3

First Printing, October, 1980

1   2   3   4   5   6   7   8   9

PRINTED IN THE UNITED STATES OF AMERICA

TO
JEAN RICKARD

THANKS!

THE SONG SAYS, "If they asked me, I could write a book." In my case, I can write a book if I ask friends. There cannot be many authors lucky enough to have such good friends who are also such able editors and so generous with their time.

My associate, Jean Rickard, not only goes over everything I do, marking what to Save, what to Toss, and what Needs More Work—she has also been more responsible than anyone else for the organization, makeup and production of this book. She and my longtime friend Ed Rickard have, in fact, literally made it possible.

Colleagues Bob Asher and Robin Meszoly, up to their ears in their own writing and editing work, went over every chapter in each of its many incarnations without saying "Good grief, here it comes again." They were not only enormously helpful but always managed "one more time" to take a fresh look and come up with just the right suggestions and touch-ups.

Doree Lovell, undaunted by previous experiences with my books, went over everything with her keen journalistic eye and unerring instinct for words, phrases, and meanings; and I'm indebted to her again.

Jill Stanley should get a detective's gold badge for ferreting out facts, figures, articles, records, and transcripts—as well as helping with the organization of the book.

Dan Balz, in the midst of editing, writing, and traveling during a hectic political year, took time out to go over the entire manuscript. There were other co-workers who were kind enough to go over individual chapters on which they have special information. Like, for example— Jim Hoagland, Morton Mintz, Bob Kaiser, J. W. Anderson, Mike Causey, Ron Kessler, Mark Shields, Peter Osnos, Bill Branigin, Jim Clayton, Frank Swoboda, Tim Robinson, John F. Berry, and John M. Berry.

I know, I know—all this sounds like the way actors sometimes rattle on during Oscar night, when you feel like crying "Enough yet!"

I wish I could express my appreciation in better words. I'd have them if I could have submitted this first to some of the people I'm trying to thank.

—H.B.

CONTENTS

INTRODUCTION

My name is Herbert Block. I draw cartoons and sometimes write books, and I'm very glad to meet you.

VIEW FROM YESTERDAY

HISTORY DOESN'T REPEAT itself exactly. And it's not quite true that the more things change the more they remain the same. But things do have a way of coming back from time to time.

Take men's neckties. When the mysterious people who decide such things determine the latest width for ties, it's not precisely the same as the ones you were finally getting ready to toss out. But some of them can be recycled.

A bottle of aspirin now comes in a box which advertises: EASY-OPEN CAP. It's a brand-new return-to-the-old-screwtop cap. This was in general use until the rage to top all drug bottles with adult-proof caps, which can only be opened by children, who have lots of time and curiosity. Depending on whether or not there are kids in the house, you now have a choice between the old cap and the older one.

Every once in a while I have a hunch for a cartoon sketch that fits a current situation but that seems all too familiar. As the newspapers slide across my desk, some days I feel the office is a room with déjà vu. ■

Smokesky The Bear
2/4/70

Salt
5/5/71

**"It Says Here That We're Facing An
Energy Crisis"**
12/14/72

6/7/73

**"Shh! If You Displease Them, They Might
Not Let Us Give Them Any More Special
Bargain Wheat Deals"**
10/10/73

"Wow!"
12/19/73

"When Do You Pass The Word To Him?"
12/26/73

1/11/74

"There's Always A Bright Side—We Don't Need The Car To Take Home Our Groceries Any More"
3/10/74

"What Was Your House Going To Be Made Of?"
5/30/74

3

"Last Year You Said You Were Going To Cut Down"
10/1/74

"Could We Have Guessed Wrong Somewhere?"
11/29/73

"Patience—It Can't Keep On Burning At This Rate"
8/4/74

"We Made It Over That Bridge All Right"
11/10/74

"Baby, It's Cold Inside"
3/5/75

"What Are Those Kids Playing With Down There?"
10/19/75

11/13/75

11/30/75

LONG LONG AGO

SCI-FI GUYS write about time warps. Actually, there's a time warp-and-woof, with the threads of memory running short in one way and long in another.

If some events of a dozen or more years ago seem like yesterday, other more recent ones seem long ago and far away.

Take Watergate.

By now, there is a common impression that the break-in at that building and subsequent cover-up were the extent of the Nixon administration misdeeds. This incident was merely the loose thread, or tape, that began unraveling the massive corruption and widespread scandals. A long roll call of figures from that administration either went to jail or plea-bargained in the conspiracies, frauds, violations of rights, financial hanky-panky, and other illegalities that characterized Nixon's term in office.

But now when you turn on your radio or TV, you are likely to find many of those same people appearing as authors, celebrities, or commentators. Nearly all of them, if their previous connections are mentioned, explain that they were the victims of injustice who nevertheless bore up nobly. And they are usually not pressed about their previous roles by the host-interviewers, who seem happy to be on a first-name basis with these guests.

You would think that all the administration events of the early seventies had never occurred, were a set of misprints—or that it was the press and prosecutors who had somehow covered up the truth.

Somebody at the time of Watergate spoke of having lost his moral compass. To make sure that compasses don't all get lost or mislaid—or that all the events we thought happened were not a dream—it's helpful to see some occasional update on that period. Fortunately, new information turns up from time to time.

Among the many cartoons I did about the Nixon administration's attacks on the media—which began about the time of Vice-President Agnew's speech of 1969—there were some on the attempts to control public broadcasting.

The official story at the time was that the government was simply trying to put greater control of broadcasting into the hands of local stations—performing a grass-roots community service, as it were. Of course, most local stations were not equipped with the personnel, resources, or national scope to delve deeply into government or to bring to wide attention views the administration did not want to see expressed.

In 1979, news and trade publications obtained—through the Freedom of Information Act—documents from the White House Office of Telecommunications Policy for 1969 to 1974. These documents disclosed many items not previously aired. Among them:

In a "Confidential, Eyes Only" memorandum, Nixon learned that Robert MacNeil and Sander Vanocur were going to be anchormen on a weekly program. He blew up and ordered that all funding for the Corporation for Public Broadcasting (CPB) be halted. When it was explained to him that this was not possible because of existing law and current funding already made, his staff drew up plans to localize public broadcasting.

Several memos to Nixon aide H. R. Haldeman from T. Clay Whitehead, White House Director of Telecommunications Policy, reported on the progress of efforts to discredit MacNeil and Vanocur: "We planted with the trade press the idea that their obvious liberal bias would reflect adversely on public television." In another memo: "We will quietly encourage station managers around the country to put pressure on CPB to put more balance in their programming or risk the possibility of local stations not carrying these programs."

Another Whitehead memo said that the President agreed with a

Violence On Television
4/19/73

"You're Not Thinking Of Walking Out On Us, Are You?"
2/4/75

strategy of "professing First Amendment goals in broadcasting," while "working in private to get more exercise of local broadcast responsibility."

A largely successful effort was made to control management of the Corporation for Public Broadcasting. Henry Loomis, president of CPB, gave Whitehead reports on board meetings and wrote on one of them: "This is our 'burn before reading document.' No one here knows you have it."

In the same campaign to control public broadcasting, a memo from Charles Colson told staff members not to state their plans "so explicitly" in memos. "This is a serious mistake for whatever records this piece of paper might ultimately end up in or, perish the thought, should it get out."

Perish the thought.

A more widely aired view, and one that recalled the old days, came in an interview with Senator Barry Goldwater on CBS's "Sixty Minutes" in March, 1980. Said Senator Goldwater: "Mr. Nixon hurt the Republican party and he hurt America. And, frankly, I don't think he should ever be forgiven. He came as close to destroying this country as any one man in that office ever has come."

Goldwater told of one morning when he was a guest on a television show. Talking about Nixon, at the time of the former President's second trip to China, Goldwater said, "Something just came through my mind, just like in a millisecond, 'This guy's dishonest.' And I said so."

He said so right there on television—with nothing Confidential or Eyes Only about it.

And not so long ago. ■

"You Know Where We Went Wrong? We Didn't Try To Steal The U.S. Government"
1/30/75

"I Plead Guilty On Five Counts— But Only To Protect My Good Name"
3/14/75

**"The Interesting Thing Is . . . So Many Of
Them Are In On It. They're All Coming
Out Of The Woodwork"**
—*Nixon, on Japanese involved in Lockheed bribes.*
2/25/76

**"Do You Think The Free Trip Is Enough,
Or Should We Give Him A Little
Something Extra?"**
2/27/76

5/3/77

**"And With Each Of These We Give A
Bag Of Salt"**
2/19/78

9

NEW HIGH PRICES!
NEW LOW VALUES!

WITH SOME FLUCTUATIONS, financial experts long warned us that the dollar was in trouble. I can tell them about that dollar—it hasn't been a good product.

The Treasury tried to promote a two-dollar bill that we didn't want, and then it came up with the Susan B. Anthony dollar, which—as some kind of a Treasury inside joke—was coined in almost the exact size, shape, and heft as a quarter. These have been the Edsels of currency. Meanwhile, among the items that continue to circulate are dollar bills that are practically falling apart—limp, worn things that look as if people had been wiping their kids' noses with them. Dollars like that suffer from Dangerfield's complaint—they don't get no respect.

Of course, dollars circulate more and faster these days, but that's no excuse. The Treasury is always thinking up chintzy ways of saving a few bucks on the production of bucks themselves. There have even been stories (serious) that it is considering making plastic currency that will last longer. If that doesn't work, they could go to kitchen-sink washers—if the washers aren't by that time worth more than the dollars.

Most products and services aren't what they ought to be, and the quest for the fast buck results in all our bucks going too fast. The ultimate built-in-obsolescence item has been our currency.

We didn't need to wait for people abroad to spurn our dollars. We should have known we were in trouble when salespeople in the U.S., on being presented with cash instead of credit cards, began asking for a driver's license and two other ID's. One large New York department store actually began asking cash-paying customers to supply their names and home addresses.

As for the government saving itself some cash, it can start by getting rid of the employees who keep coming up with those funny-money ideas. These are like the fun-day-Monday holidays that Congress put through—such as moving Columbus Day on the calendar so that it is then observed in some places on one day and on another day elsewhere. For a time they were able to move Veterans Day from the meaningful November 11 (World War I Armistice Day) to some Monday in October.

If left unchecked, those same people will make Halloween a national

"You Want A Chocolate Bar, Kid?"
3/2/78

8/11/78

"So Far, So Good"
1/7/79

**"It May Be The End Of Civilization As
We Have Known It"**
5/20/77

holiday—and will move it to the first Monday after the first Tuesday in February. Christmas will be the second Monday after Thanksgiving. And Thanksgiving will be the first Monday *before* Thanksgiving. The Fourth of July will be the third Monday in May. Election Day will, of course, be changed to the first Monday after Most People Go Away on Vacation.

It is only one person's opinion—or, as you might put it in double-digit figures—my twenty-two cents' worth. But I think the dollar began to slide when a lot of other things began sliding too—like those drifting holidays that came loose from their moorings.

Take the automobile, for example. People have said it many times, but this once-proud example of American ingenuity skidded into a ditch. It slipped between being not made as good as it used to be and not being in tune with new wants and needs.

Can you blame a lot of those dollars for running off in Japanese and German cars?

I don't discount the effect of foreign oil prices in our downward economic slide—or the fact that rulers of a few backward countries decided to make more and faster bucks than anybody had thought possible.

But statesmanship has gone through a devaluation as well. In our own

"Now That You're Not Selling So Many,
Maybe You Could Try Making Them Better"
5/22/75

"I Hardly Got It Shoveled Out Of The Snow
Before I Lost It In A Pothole"
2/27/79

government all three branches have been giving us a good deal less than the best.

In 1976 we were still getting a lot of inflated promises. We don't need any more of those, and we don't need protectionist politicians who blame our troubles on foreign imports, like autos and TV sets. Many of these are among the best made. So are some of the imported TV programs and movies.

I don't think we should spurn products that do not salute and sing "The Star-Spangled Banner." And I don't think it improves our job situation to buy only American and thus encourage other countries to buy only non-American. It's no good saying that all these products from abroad are based on cheap labor either, because they're not. Pay scales in some other countries have surpassed ours. Those other countries were number two, three, four, and elsewhere down the line, and they tried harder.

Where we probably excel is in TV and radio commercials, which cost more per minute than the shows they interrupt, and which seem to keep coming with greater frequency. They alternate with network "promos" —promoting the shows coming up for the rest of that night, the next night, and forever All this has something to do with "ratings," which

"They Keep Getting Hungrier"
6/24/77

"This Is Our Big Chance To Compete—
We'll Raise Our Prices Too"
11/19/78

have nothing to do with whether TV fare is first-rate or fourth-rate.

About ratings—they need a new category or two for movies, now largely classified PG, R, and X. There should be a BG rating for blood-and-gore pictures, and maybe an H for horror. In the movies I don't particularly care to see people come apart, or to all but feel the blood spurting in my eye. That's entertainment? Also I am not fascinated by death—either the "living dead" or the dead dead. If I wanted to be a surgeon or a coroner, I'd go to medical school instead of the movies.

Depreciation in dollars, in products, and in entertainment has also extended to education. Here it is not a case of the fast buck but of the fast bucking-the-kid-along-to-the-next-grade. It produces graduates who can hardly make their way through a phone book or figure the cost of four twenty-five-cent items in a grocery store. This decline in education is partly caused by a willingness to skip standards in order to keep things moving. In some schools, teacher may be willing to promote an undeserving kid because if he doesn't, the kid might beat up teacher.

So everybody is moved along like guests at the Mad Hatter's tea party.

One thing that is not moving right along is the U.S. mail, where for $7.50 they will now guarantee the overnight service we used to get for six cents. And for $2 we can get the "Special Delivery" we used to get for fifteen cents—except that it now takes a day or two longer than regular mail.

Item: Survey Shows Drop In TV Viewing
12/20/77

"It's My Own Invention . . . You See I Carry It Upside-Down, So That The Rain Can't Get In"
—*Through The Looking-Glass*
4/21/76

14

Another non-mover is our transportation system. Our railroads are the non-envy of all the advanced countries in the world; we have rolling stock that is also a laughing stock. This is partly because our transportation system has been built around and under the individual motor vehicle, through enormous funds allocated to the highway lobby.

We have bigger and longer highways for bigger and heavier trucks, and for passenger vehicles too. It's a big country, but most of the driving is not done on the once-in-a-lifetime trips to make sure the kids see Yellowstone. There's a lot of stop-and-go driving to the store for a pack of almost anything. It would not be too hard to design smaller (and cheaper) vehicles, similar to golf carts, for smaller trips. Urban mass transit and railroads would go a long way to solving our energy-transportation problem. Improving railroads would cost money. But the

"Read Me What It Says, Dad"
6/8/77

Escalator Education
9/25/77

**"We Already Have Something Going
Down That Road"**
9/14/77

"Brilliant Planning"
5/8/79

**"Oh, Dandy—Just What We've
Been Needing"**
2/13/75

16

highways and the aid-to-Chrysler and a lot of other things that soak up federal subsidies also cost money.

Subsidies to airlines cost money too. In the air traffic department, defective planes need to be made safer, and something also needs to be done to untangle the overcrowded and dangerous airports to make arrivals and departures safer too.

A prime example of the Backward March of Progress is the public transportation between New York City and Washington, D.C. There was a time when you could go from one city to the other to see an evening play or attend a dinner and then catch a train or plane at, say, midnight or 1:00 A.M., for the return home. The planes and trains don't run that way any more. This generally means hotel accommodations, an early dash for plane or train, and a late start to work the next day.

The passengers these days have to start the dash for the plane earlier than they used to if they care about getting a seat.

In 1978, the Civil Aeronautics Board, under the chairmanship of Alfred Kahn, deregulated the airlines—a move supposed to provide

2/14/79

**Greatest City In The Greatest Nation
In The World**
7/15/77

**"You May Tell The FPC That We've Already
Developed A New Backup System"**
8/5/77

**"I Can't Wait To See This Year's New
Line Of Excuses"**
1/10/75

**"They Just Recalled My Tires Too—And
I'm Thinking Of Leaving The Body
To Science"**
5/28/72

more competition in ticket pricing. This also resulted in more competition for seats and more seats jammed closer together.

Another supposed gain was the treatment of passengers who, with purchased flight tickets in hand, are told that they can't go because the plane is already full. The CAB congratulated itself for providing that all the ticket-holding passengers "bumped" in this way be given partial refunds and be put on something like the "next available flight," whenever or whatever that might be.

This whole bumping business doesn't fly.

Anyone who buys a ticket for a specific flight and shows up at the airport at a reasonable time should be sure of a seat on that flight. That's the one you bought the ticket for. Why shouldn't you be on it? Well, because airlines overbook flights—often selling tickets to far more

"... One Nation ... Indivisible ..."
2/22/77

people than they can accommodate. This is to make sure they have a full flight even when "no-shows" don't show.

There's a simple solution, but one which eluded Mr. Kahn and the CAB. When people buy tickets they don't use, they can be given only a partial refund—however partial necessary to discourage "over-buying." But the airlines feel it is easier to punish many of the passengers who show up on time than to penalize those who don't.

In too many cases today, services are not very good. When we buy products at stores, we generally find ourselves put on hold for some "next available" delivery—if they deliver at all.

Names of service people who do a decent job at a decent rate are passed along to special friends like information slipped around by members of an underground.

We've had a kind of service-related inflation-recession in which we pay more and more dollars for less and less quality.

We need to stop letting our values be marked down, taking whatever we can get "as is," with service that's not as was, and at prices that never were. ■

Unsafe At Any Level
1/2/76

"If You Have To Ask, You Can't Afford It"
2/2/79

"I Think They Must Have Deregulated The Seating Space First"
11/12/78

21

MAJESTY OF THE LAW

A STORY IS TOLD about the famous 19th-century senator William Hart Benton being honored at a dinner where the speakers outdid each other in praising him. They went from the flowery to the ornate to the extravagant to the blindingly splendid. He was the greatest of statesmen, a paragon so brilliant and shining that he practically illuminated the universe. When they finished and it came his turn to speak, Benton began, "You do me but simple justice."

What most of us would like from our legal system is simple justice, and it needn't be fancy or flowery. But what grinds through the courts is frequently not simple and all too often what comes out is not justice. The lady with the blindfold may be lucky if she does not also have her hands tied and her feet measured for cement shoes.

Let the reader do some judging of his own.

Case one:

During the night of March 15, 1975, a woman alone in an apartment in Alexandria, Virginia, heard a knock on her door. When she asked who it was, a man's voice answered, "The FBI." When she asked for identification, she was told to open the door. Alarmed, she ran to phone for help, as the man and the others accompanying him began breaking in. Frightened and in tears, she finally unlocked the door; and the men, armed with revolvers and shotguns, burst in and placed her under guard.

You might think this was a terrorist raid similar to the one in which Patty Hearst was abducted. Not so. The men who held the woman prisoner and searched her apartment for a quarter of an hour before producing credentials were FBI men and local plainclothes police, who were *looking* for Patty Hearst. They did not produce a warrant.

This break-in, in response to an anonymous phone call, was defended by FBI Director Clarence Kelley. He said the anonymous call had a "definite air of authenticity"—and the agents could not show their identification cards because there was not enough space to slide a card beneath the door. (This feat was later performed by a reporter with no difficulty.)

The woman, Elizabeth Ann Norton, twenty-one, was so severely shaken that she left her job in Washington and returned to her home in

"Oh, Stop Thinking About It—As Long
As We're Never Kidnaped, We Can Assume
We'd Behave Better Than She Did"
3/24/76

"Right, Chief—Patty Hearst Can't Make
Fools Of Us"
4/9/75

"Next Case"
12/5/78

"If Our Men Had Showed An Identification
Card, How Do We Know She Wouldn't
Have Swiped It?"
3/21/75

**"I've Solved The Crime Problem—
If You'll Get In There, It'll Be Easier To
Protect You"**
1/16/76

"I Never Tire Of Watching Them"
7/9/78

**"It's Your Own Fault For Being Built
That Way"**
6/1/77

3/30/78

West Virginia. She also filed suit on the grounds that her constitutional rights had been violated. U.S. District Judge Robert R. Merhige ruled that the officers had acted illegally and that the government should pay Miss Norton the modest sum of $12,500. But Judge Merhige was later overruled by the U.S. Fourth Circuit Court of Appeals, which held that while her rights had admittedly been violated, she could not collect damages unless she could prove the agents had acted in bad faith.

Miss Norton carried her case to the Supreme Court. "I don't want to see this country turn into a police state," she said. "Sometimes I think I should have kept my mouth shut, but now I'm prepared to fight it as far as I can."

The case was important because it involved the issue of illegal acts by law enforcement officers against innocent citizens.

But the issue had somehow become transformed. It was no longer the protection of a person's constitutional right to be secure in her home. It had become the protection of government agents acting ("in good faith") without a warrant.

In December, 1978, more than three and a half years after the break-in which resulted in Miss Norton's breakdown, the Supreme Court declined to review the ruling against her. The government and its agents were protected, but not the woman whose home they had invaded.

Next case:

Here we have Linda Sparkman of Kendallville, Indiana, who in 1971 —at the age of fifteen—was sterilized without her knowledge. Linda's mother claimed that the girl (then unmarried) had gone out with men, sometimes all night. She asked a local judge, Harold D. Stump, to approve the sterilization. This he did, in secret, without the girl's knowledge, and without giving her an opportunity to get legal counsel or to have any kind of a hearing.

A physician cooperated in this charade, telling the girl that she was entering the hospital for an appendectomy. Her appendix was taken out when the sterilization was performed.

A couple of years later, Linda married. In time, she and her husband worried about her inability to conceive. Eventually the facts surfaced and the physician acknowledged the secret operation.

Mrs. Sparkman and her husband sued her mother, the judge, the physician, and the medical assistants.

Mrs. Sparkman's suit reached the court of federal judge James E. Eachbach, who dismissed it on the grounds that Judge Stump was "clothed with absolute judicial immunity"—as if his robe were a kind of magic garment. This ruling was reversed by the U.S. Seventh Circuit Court of Appeals, which used the term "tyranny from the bench" in pointing out that Judge Stump did not possess absolute power. It also cited a state law designed to protect even institutionalized persons against such procedures.

The case went to the Supreme Court, where Justice Potter Stewart asked the defense attorney what would happen to a judge who granted a mother's request that her daughter's hands be cut off because the child was a shoplifter. Would such a judge be immune from suit? Justice Stewart pointed out that there was "no case, no litigants and not even the pretext of principled decision-making."

But a 5-3 majority of the Supreme Court justices held that Judge Stump's secret and unrecorded approval of a mother's request for the sterilization of a fifteen-year-old girl was a judicial act—"one normally performed by a judge."

So much for the rights of a minor.

A more recent case, in June, 1979, involved a less permanent loss but one treated by the Supreme Court in an equally cavalier manner. A man in Texas had been arrested by mistake but kept locked up for three days in one jail and five days in another while he protested the error. Eventually a check of photos and other identification proved him right. But the Supreme Court, by a 6-3 vote, felt the matter to be of no consequence—a mere eight days of false imprisonment was not a sufficient amount of time to be considered a violation of constitutional rights.

"Now Get Out Of The Car And Don't
Ask Any Questions"
12/7/77

4/17/80

Justice William Rehnquist expressed certainty that detention over a New Year's weekend did not amount to deprivation of liberty without due process of law. Happy New Year, if not happy new definition of liberty and due process.

Some imperious rulings recall a story told about Mussolini who was chatting with a visitor when his speeding limousine struck a man. The dictator is supposed to have shrugged and said, "What is the life of an individual in the affairs of a state?"

In a 1977 decision involving the rights of individuals and the rights of "the authorities," the issue was the right of a policeman to require occupants to step out of a car, even when only a minor traffic violation was involved.

The actual case involved two men in an auto with expired license tags and two Philadelphia policemen who asked the driver to get out of the car and present his registration and driver's license.

The Supreme Court reversed a Pennsylvania supreme court ruling and decided 5-3 in favor of general "stop-and-frisk operations," though dissenting Justice John Paul Stevens held that there should be "an articulable reason to suspect criminal activity . . . to justify a stop and frisk."

In the Philadelphia police case, it turned out that both men in the car were carrying concealed weapons.

One of the arguments for unlimited stopping-and-frisking is that

The New Permissiveness
6/22/73

"That's To Take Care Of Obscenity Cases"
5/27/77

many officers have been shot while approaching parked cars. Indeed they have, usually by people who don't wait to be asked to get out of their cars before opening fire.

But what about the non-criminal who may be guilty of a petty infraction of rules? Let us suppose—as I have in a nearby cartoon—that you are a woman driving down a lonely road. You are instructed by a man, or men, who may or may not be in uniform, to stop and get out of your car. This, in fact, recalled the operating procedure of a Maryland rapist who put a flashing red light atop his car. State troopers warned women to beware.

So in your car you are somewhat in the position of the woman who was told by a male voice to open her apartment door.

Court rulings do not run entirely in one direction. In April, 1980, Justice Stevens wrote a 6-3 decision (Chief Justice Warren Burger, Justices Byron White and William Rehnquist dissenting) requiring that except in certain emergencies police must obtain a warrant before entering a home. This affirmation of individual rights was worth a cheer, but the general trend of the Burger Court decisions was away from protection of citizens from intrusion.

However, that Court was determined to protect individuals from themselves—particularly from things that might appeal to "prurient interests."

In June, 1973, the Supreme Court decided to settle the difficult matter of obscenity once and for all. Some Court rulings are referred to as "landmark decisions." The Burger Court produced what might be called a "quagmire decision." While previous courts had sought to avoid entering "political thickets," this one stepped boldly into a political-legal-pornographic morass and sank in up to its eyebrows.

The opinion of the Court majority included all four Nixon-selected members of the Court plus Justice White. In his majority opinion, Chief Justice Burger wrote of "the obscenity problem" that ". . . today, for the first time since Roth was decided in 1957, a majority of this Court has agreed on concrete guidelines to isolate 'hard-core' pornography from expression protected by the First Amendment . . ."

It spelled out its definition of "hard-core" pornography. It also held that to be classified as obscene, material need no longer be *utterly* without redeeming social value (an earlier criterion) if the work seemed to lack any serious literary, artistic, political, or scientific value—and if it appealed to "prurient interest" and portrayed sexual conduct in a "patently offensive manner."

But the real kicker in this decision was the ruling that obscenity would be judged in relation to "community standards."

What community? What standards? Queens County? Salt Lake City?

XXX RATED

Supreme Court To Rule Again On "Obscenity" And "Community Standards"

Thesaurus

U.S. Atlas and Guidebook

Dictionary

©1977 HERBLOCK

"Nine, Please"
11/9/77

29

"Private Citizen"—1977
7/14/77

"I Like This Robe-And-Dagger Stuff"
2/22/80

"Think It Needs Some More Adjusting?"
3/18/77

Personal Profile
1/12/77

The state of Texas? Amityville? Madison Avenue? The area within sound of Capistrano's mission bells?

Obscenity (and the punishment for publishing it) was now to be decided by local prosecutors, local judges, and local juries whose decisions would reach far beyond their own vague "communities."

Thus, Harry Reems, who performed for one day in Miami, Florida, in the filming of the movie *Deep Throat*, was tried and convicted in Tennessee because a print of the movie had been shipped there.

Larry Flynt, of *Hustler* magazine—published in Columbus, Ohio—was indicted, tried, and convicted in Atlanta, Georgia.

Today a person who publishes a magazine or acts in a film made in New York or Miami can wonder if he will pay in Peoria—with a trial and jail sentence.

Among the dissenters in this pornography case, at least one justice had noted in a prior decision that obscenity cases had become a "burden" on the Court, and the examination of the contested materials "is hardly a source of edification to the members of this Court."

Justice William O. Douglas, in dissent, held that the First Amendment was not meant to exclude what someone somewhere might find obscene, and felt no need to spend his time watching the skin flicks at all.

Citing the majority's tests for obscenity, which include depicting or describing sexual conduct "in a patently offensive way," Justice Douglas found such tests themselves "offensive." He wrote, "Obscenity—which even we cannot define with precision—is a hodge-podge. To send men to jail for violating standards they cannot understand, construe and apply is a monstrous thing to do in a nation dedicated to fair trials and due process . . ." Justice Douglas wrote further:

> The idea that the First Amendment permits government to ban publications that are "offensive" to some people puts an ominous gloss on freedom of the press. That test would make it possible to ban any paper or any journal or magazine in some benighted place . . . The use of the standard "offensive" gives authority to government to cut the very vitals out of the First Amendment. As is intimated by the Court's opinion, the materials before us may be garbage. But so is much of what is said in political campaigns, in the daily press, on TV, or over the radio. By reason of the First Amendment—and solely because of it— speakers and publishers have not been threatened or subdued because their thoughts and ideas may be "offensive" to some.

In formulating the majority opinion, Chief Justice Burger recognized the futility of requiring "a State to structure proceedings around evidence of a *national* community standard."

In narrowing the area of judgment to the community, I think he was on the right track, but he didn't go far enough.

The proper unit for determining what a person should be allowed to see and hear is not the federal government, not the state government, the county, city, community, or precinct, but the individual adult. No government should force him to see and hear what he doesn't want to. No government should prevent him from seeing freely, or at several dollars a copy, whatever shows and publications he chooses.

As the nation celebrated its Bicentennial, the Supreme Court seemed more than 200 years away from the founders' ideas of the relationship of the individual to the state.

The Blob
11/28/75

One of the Court's 1976 rulings held that police may circulate arrest records and mug shots of people never convicted of crimes—with no risk of being held accountable in federal court.

In another decision, the Court ruled that prosecutors have absolute immunity from civil suits in federal court for knowingly using perjured testimony to convict an innocent person.

The Court also held that despite a consistent pattern of police abuses, federal judges could not require police to improve their procedures for dealing with citizen complaints.

The Court's decisions have not only affected the citizen's relationship to government but to non-public institutions as well.

By limiting class-action suits, the Burger Court reduced the power of individuals to challenge big business practices.

In this respect it has been willing to leave the individual very much on his own—to try to balance his personal legal resources against those of a large institution.

However, when it comes to privacy, the individual is not alone at all. He is on public record and open to inspection.

The Court, again in 1976, held that a person's bank records belong to the bank. Customers have "no legitimate expectations of privacy" (a favorite term of this Court) in their bank transactions. The Court also added that neither banks nor government agents need inform customers when their records have been seized or inspected.

This decision was in keeping with the spirit of the days of the founders only to the extent that in those times people were more likely to keep their money in grandfather clocks or at the bottom of trunks. In present-day America, what can a person do to keep his personal records personal? If you were to ask a policeman whether you should keep your spare cash in the bureau drawer, he would probably think you were almost as much a fool as if you asked whether you should open your door to unidentified men.

Under the rulings of the Burger Court, we are in danger of becoming like the sad lady in the play who "always depended on the kindness of strangers." And frequently they don't even knock. ■

THE OPEN
AND CLOSED SOCIETY

YOU CAN'T TRUST too much in signs. Some that look unmistakably clear are less reliable than signs of the zodiac. There is, for example, the card in the restaurant or shop window that says in large black letters: OPEN —even when the place is closed tight. The whole purpose of the reversible card is that it can be turned around before locking up, to read CLOSED. But it is easier to leave it in the window all the time and let the potential customer learn, by trial and error, that the sign merely means: We're open when you can get in the door.

We live in an open country, and presidents talk about conducting open administrations. But there are shifting standards about what government matters are open to the people and what personal matters are open to the government.

The press, which is in the business of letting people know what's going on, is often at odds with government officials who are more interested in getting out their own versions of what they are doing, and who deplore "leaks" that they have not leaked themselves.

In recent years, the press has been concerned about court rulings affecting it. One of these was *The Stanford Daily* case.

On April 12, 1971, following violence in a demonstration at Stanford University, Palo Alto police officers, armed with a warrant, surprised *The Stanford Daily* by entering and searching its offices. They rifled files to see if they could find any photographs which might lead to prosecutions of demonstrators. They found none.

The police had not tried to obtain a subpoena. Had they done so, there would have been no rifling of the files for a photo, if one existed. Instead, the *Daily* would have been on notice that it would have to produce such a photo unless it chose to go to court to contest issuance of the subpoena.

The Supreme Court, in a 5-3 decision, upheld the right of police to conduct such let's-look-around operations in attempts to find evidence of crimes which did not involve the persons or publications whose offices were searched.

Newspapers promptly pointed out that the effect of such rummaging would be to destroy confidentiality of memos and other material. They

"And Bring Me Their Heads So I Can See
What Goes On Inside Them"
8/31/78

"We Were Told They Were
'Strict Constructionists' "
4/7/76

"Rest Assured That I Will Give Your Little
Writing Effort Fair Consideration"
1/8/76

also noted the potential effect on future Watergates—exposures of corruption—when officials being exposed could find excuses for searching newspaper files.

But the case involved more than the "chilling effect" on the press—it put on ice everyone's reasonable right to privacy. In its efforts to help police search for anything that might relate to a crime, the Supreme Court hung an OPEN sign on the offices and homes of all people who were not under suspicion of any crime.

Such "law-and-order" rulings left previous law in disorder.

When President Nixon named his choices for four Supreme Court vacancies, he said that he wanted "strict constructionists" and a less "activist" court.

These terms are practically meaningless. If, as Charles Evans Hughes once observed, "the Constitution is what the judges say it is," a "strict constructionist" is one who construes it the way you want to see it construed. Justice Hugo Black was the strictest of "strict constructionists" on the First Amendment, which he held to be absolute.

As for "activism," a car—or a court—that runs backward is just as active as one that runs forward.

6/2/78

"Listen, Nosey—I'm Getting Damn Tired Of Your Interrupting Me While I'm Working"
5/18/78

36

What Nixon got in his four appointments was probably what a president usually wants—people who are closer to his way of thinking. In Nixon's case this meant closer to his "law-and-order" views than to previous Court positions on civil liberties.

Newspaper people have come in conflict with some courts by declining to disclose sources of information. The argument is made that every patriotic citizen should want to aid the government in pursuit of crime. That sounds fine in theory, but a free press exists to serve the people, not the state. A reporter cannot effectively do the job he's supposed to do and at the same time act as a police agent.

Members of the press do not consider themselves above the law. Many have gone to jail to protect their sources of information when they have believed confidentialities to be sufficiently important.

Another bone of contention between the press and the bar has been "pre-trial publicity." It is argued that this publicity makes it impossible

"Tell Us About The Voices That Speak To You"
12/10/72

for defendants to receive fair trials. But that common legal ploy does not seem to be borne out by the record. Defendants such as Angela Davis, whose supporters claimed that the publicity made a fair trial impossible, were acquitted—and might even have benefited from the constant cry about the impossibility of a fair trial. Maurice Stans, John Mitchell, John Connally, and others who figured prominently in the papers and on TV in connection with Watergate were acquitted in at least some of their trials. If the pre-trial publicity argument were completely valid, a person who committed a crime so monstrous that everyone heard about it would have an automatic out. He couldn't get a "fair trial" anywhere.

But when the jury system was established, the peers who were impaneled were often members of the community who knew each other, knew the basics of the case and all the rumors besides. It was never

Breaking And Entering
4/20/79

38

expected that jurors should be brought in from caves. They are not supposed to be ignorant but to be fair.

Supreme Court rulings affecting the press have reverberated in lower courts. In one 1978 case, journalists pleaded that records of long-distance calls not be given out in response to government subpoenas without giving the newspaper people some notification. A U.S. Court of Appeals ruled that there was no need for this—and no need to give the journalists a chance to seek a judicial ruling prior to the government's obtaining the phone records. The 2-1 majority said the Supreme Court had made it clear that in conducting criminal investigations, the government's needs "always override a journalist's interest in protecting his source." The Supreme Court declined to review this case, letting it stand.

Two 1979 decisions gave worrisome indications of the Supreme Court majority's attitudes on privacy and publicity—and on the authority of judges.

The first decision literally approved "breaking and entering" by police agents to plant listening devices when a tap or bug has been approved by a judge. This ruling meant that homes and offices were not secure against what was previously considered illegal intrusion.

"When People Say We're Still Wiretapping
It Makes Me So Mad I Feel Like Talking
Right Back To Them"
10/15/75

"Anything You Want, Dear"
2/14/74

The second case involved a concern for privacy of court proceedings—an issue that remained completely confused until it was partly clarified in a July, 1980 decision. The 1979 ruling included several riding-off-in-all directions opinions. Five justices held that a court pre-trial hearing could be closed to both press and public.

The majority opinion stated that the right to a public trial belonged only to the accused. But in separate opinions, others in the majority held that this decision applied only to pre-trial hearings; one member held that the press may have a First Amendment right to attend pre-trial proceedings, and another held that any judge can close any criminal proceeding without even giving a reason.

After the Court adjourned for the summer of '79, four of the members made off-the-bench public statements expressing their various views. Whatever their own disagreements, what they all had in common seemed to be an unhappiness with the press.

One justice felt that the press was crying wolf about the possibilities of closed courts—although, in the wake of the Supreme Court ruling, dozens of lower courts had already moved to close hearings and trials.

A couple of other justices asserted that some of those lower courts apparently believed too much of what they read in the newspapers—which they said inaccurately reported its opinions. The fault, dear Brutus, is not in ourselves but in our Stars, Posts, Timeses, and Tribunes. In

"Some Of You People Seem To
Be Confused"
9/16/79

"You Might Not Recognize My Face—But
With My Credit Card, You Know My
Name And . . ."
2/17/76

other words, the trouble was not with confusing Supreme Court opinions or with lower court judges who apparently weren't expected to read or understand what the Supreme Court wrote. The trouble was with the press.

The Court is not alone among government branches or agencies to find that the sins and omissions of "the media" are always greater than their own. As surely as some mystery devotees can be counted on to murmur that "the butler did it," some government officials will say, "The press is to blame!"

Even when congressional committees expose government wrongdoing, the wrongdoers are likely to cry out against the papers and broadcasts which report the committee disclosures. In 1975, when the Senate Committee headed by Frank Church held televised hearings in which the CIA did not come off very well, those who believed that secrecy means security directed much of their anger at the media.

Judges, legislators, presidents, and government agents who blame the press often go on the assumption that the press should serve as a handmaiden to government. Thus, CIA officials complained that they were injured by accounts of their mistakes, but they did not hesitate to employ some all-too-willing newspapermen to serve them—or to have CIA agents pose as newsmen—without regard to the damage done to the

"I Shot An Arrow Into The Air . . ."
1/6/78

In The Bag Of Dirty Tricks
1/25/76

reading public or to the credibility of the press. The CIA also planted phony stories in publications abroad—stories which were often picked up in American publications, and sometimes recounted in congressional debates—all of this without regard for the press, the congressmen, or the American public, who were all being misled.

As recently as April, 1980, CIA Director Stansfield Turner told editors that it was still the policy of the CIA to use American news people as CIA agents. This policy was supported by President Carter but was contrary to the policy stated by previous CIA Director William Colby.

There used to be a radio program called "I Love a Mystery"—a title which expressed a great truth. Most of us *do* love mysteries, a fact played on by every official who whispers of secrets and national security, when no security is involved beyond job security or secrecy to avoid looking silly.

Under the Freedom of Information Act, Jack Anderson got a peek at part of the dossiers the CIA had compiled on him and his staff—a file nearly four inches thick. It included a full report of a luncheon he had in a Washington hotel dining room with Richard Helms, then CIA director. The report was filed by the director's agents, who were stationed outside the hotel and at tables in the hotel dining room. If Jack Anderson had tried to assault Director Helms with a celery stalk, the agents would have

"Anchors Aweigh"
4/16/80

9/30/76

42

been on him in a flash. On any given day, as many as sixteen agents in eight cars watched columnist Anderson and his staff to study what they called "behavior patterns."

This surveillance disclosed that Anderson's associate, Les Whitten, picked up *his* lunch "to go" and ate it in Farragut Square, a public park. The report did not disclose whether Whitten's sandwich was accompained by pickles or relish—or whether the agents had any comments on the behavioral patterns of the Farragut Square pigeons.

Your tax dollars at work.

Government intelligence is necessary and not a matter to be taken lightly. That's why it should be obtained by people who *show* some intelligence. Incidentally, the CIA, which did not come into existence until after World War II, is only one of the federal government's intelligence services. But it has become the best known and the loudest in complaining that any disclosures of its mistakes and misdeeds endanger the country.

Since the 1979–80 crisis in Iran and the Russian invasion of Afghanistan, there has been a longing for some secret magic solution to our troubles abroad, and CIA hardliners have given the impression that if the agency were allowed to do as it pleased, there would be no such problems.

But the record does not support this conclusion.

Whatever intelligence we obtained before the Iranian coup, our ambassador there from 1973 to 1976 was Richard Helms, former director of the CIA. Some time after the coup, he acknowledged that perhaps more coverage of activity in the mosques and in the poorer sections might have helped.

There were no restraints on the CIA, which was riding high and feeling even higher in 1961, at the time of the Bay of Pigs disaster. That action was planned and executed by the CIA with the approval of the Eisenhower and Kennedy administrations.

As for the press, which is often accused of revealing secrets or of making more difficult the work of government, it's worth recalling the role of newspapers at that time. *The New York Times* (for one) was aware of the forthcoming invasion attempt but cooperated with the government by withholding the story. President Kennedy later told the editor that he wished *The Times* had printed its story before the blunder was committed.

Later, in hatching assassination plots against Fidel Castro, the CIA obtained outside help. It collaborated with the Mafia—another quaint method of defending the American way of life.

Investigations of these assassination plots disclosed plans that involved poisoned cigars, exploding seashells, a contaminated diving suit, a dart

"Yes, Mr. And Mrs. America—This Is Your Life"
3/28/75

gun, a poison pen, and a substance that was supposed to be put into Castro's shoes, with the ultimate effect of making his beard fall out. For those who claim that in this tough world anything is necessary that gets results, we should remember that all this fun-shop stuff—and the collaboration with the Mafia—did not work.

It is not the purpose here to go into all the activities of this agency abroad or into the question of how many congressional committees it should report to in order to work effectively. In this section on the open-and-closed society, what is of concern is the relationship of such government agencies to the American people.

George Bush, former head of the CIA, has said that we must get off the CIA's back—although that agency, in conducting illegal activities in the United States, was on the backs of Americans.

A *Washington Post* article of September 9, 1979, gave some idea of the extent of the illegal CIA activities at home. It began:

> The Central Intelligence Agency considered its spying on American political and civil rights leaders such as Sen. Robert F. Kennedy and the Rev. Martin Luther King, Jr., as having the same high priority as its intelligence gathering on the Soviet Union and Communist China, according to CIA files.

"Nope, None Of Our Business—Neither Of Them Seemed To Be Members Of The Socialist Workers Party"
8/13/76

New Library Section
12/4/75

"I'm OK—You're OK"
8/9/79

**"What You Need Is A CIA Director Who
Inspires My Confidence"**
1/28/77

12/29/74

Behavior-Altering Drug
8/9/77

These files had been turned over to plaintiffs in a civil lawsuit challenging the legality of the CIA's "Operation Chaos" domestic spying program in the late 1960s and early 1970s.

The article went on to say that as long as two years after Director Richard Helms had put Operation Chaos in the highest category (on a par ranking with Soviet and Chinese Communist data), the CIA inspector general reported "numerous signs of uneasiness over the agency's role" because Chaos "appeared to constitute a monitoring of Americans not known to be or suspected of being involved in espionage."

Helms's reaction, according to another CIA memo, was to suggest that the person heading the program continue the same operation but "become identified with the subject of terrorism" rather than "domestic spying" activities.

Helms, like some officials of the FBI, complained that the intelligence agencies suffered from the "devastating" effect of "endless incursions and inquiries" as a result of the Freedom of Information Act.

That is the Freedom of Information Act which enabled people to find out that Director Helms placed the surveillance of Robert Kennedy, Martin Luther King, Jr., Coretta King, Bella Abzug, and Congressman Ronald Dellums in the same category as obtaining intelligence on Soviet Russia. It was not surprising that Mr. Helms did not like it.

Undercover Work
1/31/75

"We Broke The Law? We Are The Law!"
4/16/78

47

"You Wished A Job Done, Sir?"
3/4/75

"Maybe That's One Reason It's Been So Slow"
3/19/75

"We Hadn't Planned To Include This In The Tour, Senator"
11/20/75

Aren't Those The Same Agents Who Were So Worried About Protest Groups?"
6/17/77

One cannot help but wonder how the CIA was weakened in its foreign intelligence work by no longer devoting so much time, effort, and public funds to spying on such American citizens. Without these activities, it should be able to concentrate on what it *ought* to be doing—and also have time to handle the Freedom of Information Act inquiries that Mr. Helms feared. Incidentally, classified information is deleted from material supplied in response to these inquiries.

The FBI, which also engaged in illegal activities, should now be able to handle more information requests—and catch more criminals too.

One other thing—whenever we learn of abuses in the FBI, the CIA, Army intelligence, the IRS, or some other agency, we always hear that, "Ah, these things happened in the past." Since it's difficult to report on events in the future, of course the misdeeds disclosed are likely to be in the past. But that doesn't necessarily mean there is nothing more to be disclosed.

In July, 1978, the House Assassinations Committee discovered that a CIA man, a liaison officer supposedly there to assist the committee, had rifled some of the committee's files on the assassination of President Kennedy. He left photographs in disarray and his fingerprints everywhere, including the inside of the safe in which the pictures were kept. The CIA maintained that he had not been in the safe, but that he had done "some-

"That's All For Now—We'll Be Back Later"
7/6/79

"Don't Worry. This Time You Can Really Trust Me"
2/18/76

thing dumb" and that he had been fired. No further explanation of the incident was given. Another little mystery.

The FBI is supposed to have cleaned up its act, and following J. Edgar Hoover, almost any change would have been an improvement. His hatred of blacks, his use of information for personal purposes, his concoctions of anonymous letters and planted stories—literally to destroy the reputation and lives of honest people—all testified to his corruption by power.

The Jean Seberg story, which came out after her death, provided an example of his methods. The actress, who donated to many civil rights organizations, had made a contribution to the Black Panthers. When she was pregnant in 1970, Hoover planted stories, which were picked up in newspaper and magazine columns, that the baby Miss Seberg carried was not her husband's but that of a Black Panther leader. Miss Seberg, distraught over the stories, lost the baby in a miscarriage and made annual suicide attempts. She was found dead in September, 1979. In this case, Hoover did not have to try to implant the idea of suicide—as he attempted to do with Martin Luther King.

The J. Edgar Hoover FBI Building was finished and dedicated after Hoover's death and after his misdeeds were well known. His name, as

The Trouble With Cutting Corners
12/5/75

"Something Went Wrong Here"
7/13/75

"Except For Those Of Us Who Are Above It"
11/2/77

51

part of that title, is a public disgrace. It would be comparable to installing a sign on the White House calling it the Richard M. Nixon House for Presidents.

The White House is the White House, the Department of Justice is called the Department of Justice, and the building occupied by the FBI—which comes under the Department of Justice—should be simply the FBI building. That would help to renew public faith in this bureau and in the government.

When he was attorney general, Griffin Bell was concerned about FBI violations of the law—but he was also concerned about what he called the morale of the agents, his employees.

For the widespread lawbreaking which had been committed by FBI agents, Bell decided not to prosecute the men at the lower level, because they were, as the saying goes, just following orders. Bell finally decided to prosecute only three who had held positions of top responsibility. By early 1980, their trials were still being postponed because of the question of what evidence might be admitted.

The catch on prosecuting top officials was that they could practice "graymail"—by demanding to introduce into court material which the

"We Might As Well Be Consistent"
3/23/78

"How Do You Expect Our Men To Give Patriotic Dedicated Service If You Require Them To Obey The Laws?"
4/17/77

Department of Justice wanted to keep classified. In other words, they might save their hides by, in effect, threatening to spill secrets.

We have seen the Pentagon Papers and much other secret information which was supposed to threaten the Republic. And it didn't.

The disclosures of FBI information that is classified pose less of a danger to the country than the fact that FBI officials are classified as being above the law.

Between the Supreme Court's 1979 "closed court" ruling and its 1980 decision for "open trials," some justices pooh-poohed the idea that decisions on open or closed cases could have anything to do with "Watergates." They were wrong. The combination of great secrecy and great power was corrupting to the Nixon administration and to the FBI and the CIA. And it would be corrupting to the courts.

In an open society the conduct of officials in their public duties has to be open for public inspection. ■

"I'm Okay—I Can Handle It Now"
2/19/80

ONLY LIFE AND DEATH

EVERY SO OFTEN reporters interview people who live to be over a hundred, and ask, "To what do you attribute your longevity?" The answers provide no useful pattern. One person is a complete abstainer, another takes to the jug regularly; some exercise, some sit and rock. One centenarian responded to the question: "Every night I wash all over with good brandy, then I put on a clean suit and go to bed." His formula didn't produce a cult, but perhaps that was only because the brandy manufacturers and clothing makers didn't pick up on it.

Food and beverage companies generally come across louder and clearer in their advertising commercials than they do in the fine print on their labels, which list ingredients and are unspecific about what quantities of what items are in the product.

Readers of *Alice in Wonderland* will recall her finding a bottle with a label that said DRINK ME "beautifully printed on it in large letters." After looking to make sure that it was not marked "poison," she drank it—with remarkable effects. Ditto for the piece of cake marked EAT ME, which resulted in her opening up like a telescope.

The ads and containers in today's marketing Wonderland say, in alluring ways, "Eat me" and "Drink me," and nothing on the labels says, "Poison." But the fine print is not always enlightening, and the result of swallowing the products is not entirely predictable.

Manufacturers and chemists work to prolong the shelf life of foods, and it would be great if they would give the same thought to the non-shelf life of the consumer.

The ads for various junk foods are even more sugar-coated than the cereals on the market shelves. And both give the impression that they will have us vibrantly healthy, bursting with energy, and ready to win the decathlon.

The food and drug experts who tell us it ain't so and keep finding ingredients that might be harmful to us are bearers of bad news. Consumers sometimes regard them as spoilsports and the industries affected by their findings usually treat them as public enemies.

For years I drew cartoons about regulatory agencies as non-watching watchdogs. But when some of these agencies were finally staffed by

**"Deep Breathing Now—That's It—
Out Goes The Bad Air—In Comes
The Bad Air—"**
7/30/72

Human Sacrifice
1/26/75

DARK TUNNEL

Dark Tunnel
6/1/80

**"Could You Hurry And Find A Cure For
Cancer? That Would Be So Much Easier
Than Prevention"**
1/9/77

**. . . Tomorrow, And Tomorrow, And
Tomorrow . . .**
8/8/76

Mined Area
1/2/80

Wonders Of Modern Medicine
12/21/77

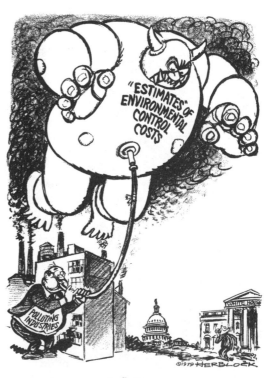

Inflation
2/28/79

people who took their work seriously, they caught a good deal more hell from other quarters. This happened with the Food and Drug Administration under the leadership of Dr. Donald Kennedy. While he was commissioner of the FDA, it became involved in the Great Saccharin Controversy.

A number of tests on laboratory mice—conducted with the high dosages usually given laboratory mice—showed saccharin to be a contributing factor to cancer. Dr. Kennedy acted to abide by the law that keeps cancer-causing products off the general food-and-drink market. An artificial sweetener lobby, with the nice healthy name of Calorie Control Council, went on the attack. The public also hollered, since

The Drums
3/21/79

Safe Level
3/30/79

"You Can't Expect Perfection"
6/7/79

**"Excuse Me—I Wonder If You'd Mind Some
Nuclear Waste In Your Neighborhood?"**
6/17/79

Three Mile Island Report
11/1/79

cyclamates had been ruled out earlier, and saccharin was the last of the synthetic sweeteners widely used in products.

There was no end of jokes about the enormous numbers of artificially sweetened sodas a mouse or a man would have to drink to produce an ill effect. And there were any number of statements and jokes about how *anything* consumed in quantity would produce cancer.

Both ideas were at odds with the facts. They demonstrated that any scientific findings (particularly involving men and mice) could produce an unlimited amount of gags.

Congress overrode the FDA and its own law in order to protect itself from public displeasure. It postponed even the partial ban on saccharin use.

When Dr. Kennedy retired from the FDA in 1979, his successor was

"You Say You Have This Tendency To Glow In The Dark?"
3/13/79

59

4/15/79

Dr. Jere Edwin Goyan, who also believed that the purpose of the agency was to regulate food and drugs. To adults who said triumphantly that they had long been using a little saccharin in their coffee, he pointed out that children today, tossing down lots of saccharin soft drinks, will absorb a great deal of the stuff in their lifetimes.

Moreover, some potentially harmful items in combination have a synergistic—or multiplying—effect. Saccharin products and cigarettes seem to be such a combination. Both are available in coin machines to everyone—including kids.

The Federal Trade Commission probably got into its biggest flap when it urged restraint in TV ads aimed at kids—especially those promoting heavily sugar-coated cereals. And when nutritionists have tried to remove candy and soft drinks from school vending machines, they have gotten a bitter reaction from all the interests involved.

As Secretary of the Department of Health, Education and Welfare, Joseph Califano found that however dangerous smoking might be to the public health, a secretary of HEW who warned of these hazards might find such efforts harmful to his political health. There were a couple of ironic incidents in the smoking controversy. A commission, sponsored by

Breeder
5/18/77

Dragon's Teeth
10/12/76

"Why Doesn't The Government Just Let Everyone Decide For Himself What's Okay To Eat And Drink?"
3/25/77

Sweet Tooth
4/2/78

"You Think It'll Sell?"
2/5/78

"They Keep Talking About Life And Death—We've Got Money At Stake Here!"
1/12/79

the tobacco industry itself, found smoking to be hazardous—while Dr. Peter Bourne, President Carter's health adviser at the time, spoke soothingly about the relaxing pleasures of smoking.

Everyone is against cancer, but there are disagreements about how to combat it.

During the Nixon administration there was much fanfare about a presidential program to attack cancer. Many scientists pointed out that this was not a "moon-shot" type of problem whose solution lay in a crash program, a presidential commission, or more expenditures to produce a "cure." The scientists proved correct. The program was more political than practical—it gave the impression of action, distributed more money around, but scored no real gain.

In recent years, more emphasis has been put on disease prevention—particularly on curbing the use of cancer-causing agents. Asbestos fibers, chemical wastes, pesticides, and various air pollutants have received more public attention, and programs to control them have received public support. This has caused some anguish to affected industries, including industrial air polluters, disposers of toxic wastes, and auto manufacturers who were as reluctant to control harmful emissions as they were to install safety devices.

In March, 1979, an accident—or series of accidents—at the Three-

"True, You Have This Breathing
Problem, But Let's Also Consider
The Python's Side—"
11/14/76

". . . An Atmosphere That Could
Support Life . . ."
8/1/76

"This Man Is Being Deprived Of His Right To Make Other People Inhale His Smoke"
7/3/77

The Left Hand And The Right Hand
6/3/77

"You Can See That I'm The Good Guy Now"
7/31/79

"I've Heard The Food Here Is Very Good. Maybe We Can Take Some Home And Taste It"
4/16/76

Mile Island nuclear power plant in Pennsylvania created a national shock wave over the dangers of radiation and the potential hazards of nuclear plants. It also raised anew unanswered questions on how and where to dispose of nuclear wastes. All over the country, state governments gave this hot item the cold shoulder.

Incidentally, by far the greatest amount of nuclear waste comes not from power plants but from the production of nuclear weapons.

One casualty of the Three-Mile Island incident was the credibility of government assurances about the safety of nuclear power production and its official downplaying of radiation hazards in general. Reassuring government statements were not helped by disclosures that some American soldiers developed leukemia after having undergone experimental

"This Here Country Ain't Big Enough For Both Of Us"
7/27/77

"This Is An Emergency—We've Got To Prevent Any Leaks Of Information!"
4/1/79

Under A Cloud
4/22/79

"To Err Is Human, To Squeeze Out Every Buck Possible Is Divine"
4/11/79

Nuclear-Age Cloud
4/3/79

training in nuclear blast areas in the United States in the 1950s. Even people who didn't take seriously laboratory tests on mice were jolted by the use of American soldiers, in effect, as guinea pigs in such tests. While the government officially denied that it caused damage to these men, some of the survivors, now ill with cancer, testified before Congress. They asked for service-connected benefits so that their families would be provided for.

During the U.S. Civil War, a general who was trying to urge his weary troops on to yet another battle is supposed to have shouted in exasperation, "Come on, men, come on! Goddammit, do you want to live *forever*?"

We don't expect to live forever. But, with the exception of some favorite habits, we'd like the government to help us avoid unnecessary hazards. And we'd like it to level with us about what we're up against. ■

11/17/76

MIDDLE MID-EAST

THE CLASSIC TALE on the strange and unpredictable Middle East is the one about the frog and the scorpion at the river bank. The scorpion asked if it could cross the river on the frog's back. When the frog expressed fear of being stung, the scorpion said, "Don't be silly. If I sting you, we'll both drown." So they started across. When they reached midstream, the scorpion stung the frog, who asked, as they both went down, "Why did you do that?" Said the scorpion, "This is the Middle East."

The dealings between most countries of this area have often been no more cooperative than the scorpion and no more stable than the shifting sands of the desert they inhabit. Among these countries—Egypt, Syria, Saudi Arabia, Iraq, Libya, Iran, Lebanon, Kuwait, Tunisia, Algeria, and Jordan—the relationships between any two have ranged from complete unity to complete enmity.

One of the few things on which the Arab countries were united was opposition to Israel.

In 1977, President Anwar Sadat of Egypt and Prime Minister Menachem Begin of Israel reached a historic breakthrough. They sat down together to talk of peace.

Both men later received the Nobel Peace Prize, and they deserved it.

But the road to peace was rocky. Even as the Nobel Prizes were awarded, peace was uncertain. The negotiations that went on for months were a diplomatic Perils of Pauline. The role of the American government in this drama was also an uncertain one—sometimes seeming to hinder and sometimes to help.

What I want to do here is give an "it-seems-to-me" rundown on the situation in that area.

Usually the best place to begin is, as the Red King said, at the beginning. But in the Middle East, wherever you come in is in the middle. The history of territories, tribes, and conflicts is so long that it virtually goes back to the biblical "In the beginning . . ."

So . . .

In the middle of the Middle East, there was Palestine, which came under British mandate after World War I.

A part of Palestine was Trans-Jordan (now Jordan), which in 1927

**"Ah, But This Rug Will Have A Special
Backing That Will Make It Impossible
For It To Be Pulled Out!"**
3/19/71

**"I've Put An End To Their Surreptitious
Eavesdropping"**
6/1/71

25-Year War
10/9/73

Long Shadow
10/18/73

became, for all practical purposes, independent. The remainder of Palestine was partitioned by the United Nations in 1947.

Part of it became Israel. The principal remaining parts were the Gaza strip (between Israel and northern Egypt) and the area generally known as "the West Bank" because it lies on the western side of the Jordan River. Gaza and the West Bank did not belong to Jordan, to Israel, or to Egypt but were to be part of another Arab state.

The UN plan was rejected by the existing Arab states. And when Israel became a nation in 1948, it was immediately invaded by the surrounding Arab countries of Egypt, Jordan, Syria, and Lebanon—as well as Iraq. The joint attempt to destroy the new nation didn't succeed, but Jordan seized the West Bank area and held onto it. Later, Jordan tried to annex this territory, but even most Arab states refused to recognize the annexation.

Egypt took the Gaza area and administered it but did not try to annex it.

Between 1948 and 1973 Israel survived four major wars. Most decisive was the 1967 "Six-Day War," which was chiefly instigated by General Gamal Abdel Nasser of Egypt. Jordan's King Hussein came in toward the end, for what he thought would be the kill. But he learned too

Gunsight
11/26/74

**"We Have Sort Of An Accord Already—
All The Countries Agree They Want
More Arms"**
2/11/75

late that Israel was winning this war also, and he lost what his grand-father had taken earlier.

At the end of the Six-Day War, it was Israel that occupied the West Bank and Gaza as well as the Egyptian Sinai, right up to the Suez Canal.

When the cease-fire lines of 1948 were drawn, no one envisioned them as being permanent or secure. And they were not.

It is hardly surprising that a small nation, only a few miles wide—an island of democracy surrounded by hostile countries—should feel anxious for secure borders.

There's a recurring story that illustrates Israel's concern for its security.

In the early 1970s, U.S. Secretary of State William Rogers had a "peace plan," which involved Israel's giving up areas it considered vital to its defense. He went to Egypt and then on to Israel and a meeting with Prime Minister Golda Meir.

As the story goes, Mrs. Meir welcomed Secretary Rogers. She asked if he would mind stepping over to a window with her before they began their discussions. Of course he'd be glad to. She pointed to a school yard

"Just Out Of Curiosity, How Is It We Never Got A Homeland During All The Years Our Arab Brothers Had The West Bank?"
9/23/77

where children were playing. He remarked on the lovely children. Mrs. Meir then asked him to look through another window at some hills. He remarked on the very pretty hills. Well, said Mrs. Meir, those schoolchildren used to live underground because enemy soldiers in those hills were shooting down at them. Those children, said Mrs. Meir, are not going to have to live underground again. Now, Mr. Secretary, what was it you came to see me about?

End of "peace plan," end of story. Whether or not it is only a story, it makes a point.

In the tangled affairs of the Middle East, Russia as well as the United States has played a part. In 1948, Russia gave early recognition to Israel, which it now views with enmity.

By and large, Russia has had good relations with the radical Arab countries, Iraq, Syria and Libya, and with the Palestine Liberation Organization (PLO). But its relations with other states in the area have fluctuated between warm and frosty.

President Nasser of Egypt and his successor, Anwar Sadat, both welcomed Russian aid. In 1970, Russian missiles and Russian pilots as well as Russian troops were reported in Egypt.

In 1972, President Sadat, angry because the USSR would not give him

"You Sure This Is All Right? It Wasn't
On Our Program"
11/16/77

"What's The Latest?"
11/20/77

the weapons he wanted, expelled some 15,000 Russians from Egypt. But he continued to receive Russian arms on a reduced basis.

In 1973, Egypt and Syria launched against Israel the Yom Kippur war —a surprise attack, which initially succeeded. Later, the Israelis gained the advantage and surrounded the Egyptian Third Army. Russia and the United States saved Sadat by bringing pressure to bear for a cease-fire before Israel could conclude the war on the battlefield. Under Sadat, Egypt felt its military valor had been proven and its honor redeemed.

In closing out this war, Secretary of State Henry Kissinger practiced step-by-step "shuttle diplomacy," bringing about truce arrangements between Israel and Egypt—later followed by Egypt's allies. But he was unable to establish peace.

The Carter administration believed in a grand design for the Middle East, in which the lions and lambs and crocodiles, frogs and scorpions and bears would all lie down together. The United States, with Russia, proposed a new Geneva conference, which would, of course, include both major powers—and later some form of PLO representation.

Israel did not care for such an everybody-get-in-the-act conference. And the thought of a meeting jointly chaired by Russians—that Sadat had booted out of his country earlier—may have helped Sadat come up with

"What Makes That Country Think
It Has A Right To Call A Conference
On Peace?"
11/29/77

"It's Entirely Up To The Peacemakers—
Whose Plans We Trust Will Fit In
With Ours"
12/16/77

a better idea. He did—and it was so audacious that it captured the imagination of a large part of the world.

Sadat offered to go to Israel.

Prime Minister Menachem Begin responded by inviting Sadat to address the Israeli parliament (the Knesset) and also invited other Arab leaders to come and confer. None of the others accepted.

On November 19, 1977, Sadat made his historic trip to Jerusalem.

The Sadat–Begin meetings and the interviews they gave on camera constituted a kind of "television diplomacy," of which Sadat proved himself a master. He was indeed a man of imagination and daring—and a complete charmer. His talk of bold initiatives, his mannerisms, his Americanese expressions were a delight—"for sure."

His trip to Jerusalem was practically the diplomatic equivalent of Lindbergh's flight to Paris.

But Carter's idea of a comprehensive settlement was so strong that less than a month after the Sadat–Begin meeting, he dispatched Secretary of State Cyrus Vance to get a pledge from Sadat that he would not negotiate a "separate peace" with Israel. Sadat agreed.

The New Pyramid Builders
12/6/77

While Sadat had become identified as *the* man of peace, Begin soon found himself cast as an intransigent.

As Sadat spoke in Washington and the capitals of Europe about his "quest for peace," his harsh references to Begin encouraged this idea. He brought public opinion to bear against Begin's government, which was being asked to make concessions to please all Arab countries.

Any criticism of Sadat could be counted on to raise more hackles than criticism of Carter. And perhaps there was some justice in this.

Columnist Clayton Fritchey did some digging to trace the history of the on-again-off-again talks between Sadat and Begin. He found that after meeting with Begin in Ismailia at the end of 1977, Sadat gave an interview printed in the Egyptian publication, *October*.

In this, Sadat said, "It had been agreed that we should deal with general principles in Ismailia," which in itself was "a very important achievement." Sadat went on: "However, what happened was something more important and greater" than this. "Begin came and brought a complete plan on withdrawal from the occupied territories . . . they went further than one could imagine . . ."

But four days later, the controlled Egyptian press was bitterly attacking Israel. Later in January, at a Jerusalem negotiating session, Sadat abruptly called home his delegation.

"Whew!"
1/4/78

"Well. I've Got To Get Tough With Somebody!"
3/12/78

This sudden scuttling of peace talks came as a surprise even to Sadat's own delegates.

Fritchey, in his column, said:

> What prompted this seemingly inexplicable change of heart? What happened between Jan. 1 and Jan. 5? In diplomatic circles, interest centers on Jan. 4 when President Carter, after a trip to Saudi Arabia, held an unplanned meeting with Sadat at Aswan.
>
> We will probably never know for certain what took place, but the present consensus is that Sadat, rightly or wrongly, got the impression that Carter, through pressure on Israel, might be able to get him a better deal than he had been prepared to settle for at Ismailia.

If Sadat and Carter were waiting for King Hussein to help in the peace effort, that help never came. Sadat was in the position of trying to negotiate for other Arabs who did not want him to negotiate for them.

Carter clearly favored Sadat as a person and was anxious to court other Arab countries. I think Carter helped to foster the impression that Begin was the obstacle to peace.

"Yoo Hoo! Somebody Looking For Me?"
5/12/78

"Easy, Now—One Step At A Time"
9/7/78

Israeli peace initiatives were brushed aside. Opposing propositions, which practically called for Israel to accept terms laid down by the nations that had tried to destroy it, were hailed as "peace initiatives." Newspapers reported that Begin constantly "rebuffed" these "overtures" or "olive branches." And our government did nothing to dispel such impressions.

Many Americans who have grown up since the 1948 war and the 1967 war have read about "occupied territory" that was "conquered by Israel." Some must have the impression that a militaristic Israel had marched forth against innocent neighbors in wars of expansion.

Begin pointed out the difficulty of making peace with leaders who refused even to talk or to recognize his nation's right to exist.

But he could hardly preface all interviews with a history of his country and its neighbors. And when Begin talked West Bank history, he based his claims on Old Testament grounds, which left most of his listeners cold.

The better claim was in recent history, which commentator George F. Will spelled out. He reminded readers that the West Bank had never belonged to Jordan and that it was hardly in Sadat's province to negotiate for it—or for anything but the Egyptian Sinai.

More than that, during all the years that Jordan held this seized land, the separate West Bank "Palestinian entity" that Arab countries were now crying for had never been set up by Jordan.

In addition, Will pointed out that Israeli settlements in the West Bank area were at least as legal as anyone else's—and probably more so.

Palestinian refugees were indeed entitled to sympathy. But they had not been taken into Arab countries, as Jewish refugees—unwelcome in Arab lands—had been taken into Israel.

Jordan's King Hussein had, in fact, rejected a separate Palestinian entity proposed by the United Arab Republic in 1960. Hussein claimed instead the allegiance of the Palestine refugees for himself. Still later, in 1974, he said it was "totally inconceivable" that Jordan and a Palestinian state could form a federation.

Hussein had, in 1970, kicked out the PLO from his country, but only because he was in danger of being overthrown by *them*. And with the usual twists and turns of Middle East kingdoms, he later supported the PLO against Israel and welcomed Yasser Arafat to Jordan.

Saudi Arabia also conspicuously failed to back the peace process, and it too supported the PLO—as did Russia. Middle East politics makes strange bedouin-fellows.

The negotiations between Egypt and Israel several times bogged down and seemed on the verge of collapse. President Carter held a Camp David "summit" with Sadat and Begin to mend the peace process fractured by his plans for a "comprehensive settlement." He later traveled to the Middle East in his own "shuttle diplomacy," which was successful.

In September, 1978, Begin and Sadat signed the Camp David framework for peace.

The Russian government and the PLO responded by issuing a joint communiqué attacking the Camp David agreements.

King Hussein of Jordan also attacked the Camp David peace effort, although Sadat later said that Hussein had contacted him at Camp David to say: "I'm ready to join now."

On March 26, 1979, Sadat and Begin came to Washington, where, on the grounds in front of the White House, they signed a formal peace treaty between the two countries.

What remained for the two to settle were issues almost entirely outside the relations between their two countries—specifically the "Palestinian problem."

Prime Minister Begin asserted that Israel had given the West Bank Arabs more autonomy and better conditions than they had received from Jordan, itself a country carved out of the Palestinian mandate and with a large Palestinian population.

However, the drums kept beating for an Arab Palestinian state. President Carter said that he knew of no government that wanted a separate "Palestinian state." However, he called for a "Palestinian homeland," made it a front-and-center issue, and gave hints of willingness to soften his opposition to the PLO.

Since Jordan and Saudi Arabia refused to join in the peacemaking

A Star Is Born
10/11/78

Two In The Bush
11/16/78

process, this left it to Begin and Sadat to try to find a solution—no easy task. In May, 1980, after a year of working on this task, negotiations were still touch and go.

Some idea of the problem might be gained from the views of Abba Eban, former foreign minister of Israel and a member of the principal party opposed to Begin. Anticipating the peace agreement, Eban wrote in 1977 that the United States "should not hurry to raise other issues" before Egypt and Israel have time to solidify their new relationship. But this was obviously with no view to skipping other problems. Said Eban:

> Israel will not realize her true vocation or rise to the full height of her own national vision until she is free from all responsibility, control or jurisdiction over the million Arabs in Gaza and the West Bank.
>
> But to make this goal feasible for any serious sector of Israeli opinion, the Arabs and the United States need a greater understanding of Israel's right to crucial changes in the pre-1967 map and to a neighbor who seeks peace and not a springboard for war.

That "springboard for war" was precisely what was being made possible by those who demanded immediate settlement of all problems without regard for Israel's security.

It would take some doing to provide "autonomy" without creating another nation—particularly a nation that would be run by a PLO

Linkage
11/22/78

"I Give Them Something, They Give Me Something"
12/19/78

79

dedicated to destroying Israel. That would hardly seem like a gain for peace.

In spite of that, people in and out of the U.S. government saw such a settlement as the key to solving all Middle East problems.

Mixed in with all this—as it seems to ooze into everything—was oil. The argument seemed to be that appeasement of the PLO and the Arab hard-line countries would somehow insure a steady friendly flow of OPEC oil at prices not unreasonably high.

If the Middle East countries act in a bizarre fashion, U.S. policy there has blended in quite well. The United States continued to bring in 10 percent of its oil imports from Libya—a country that buys arms from Russia, supports the PLO, and has provided a haven for all kinds of terrorists. Sadat described the Libyan leader Qaddafi as a madman.

Our country's thirst for and heavy consumption of oil seemed to bring on something like a case of diplomatic DT's. We set off all alarms at the Soviet approach to the Persian Gulf through Afghanistan. But with Carter going back and forth on a Palestinian "homeland," "autonomous" Arab "entity," or whatever, we were apparently unperturbed by the prospect of a PLO state—which would give Russia another wedge in an area that already contained the volatile Iraq.

During the 1978 fighting in Lebanon, the United States, along with other countries in the UN, called for Israeli withdrawal from Lebanon— where the PLO, using it as a base of operations, had helped reduce that country to a shambles.

William B. Quandt, a former member of Carter's National Security Council staff, wrote in May, 1980:

> . . . the Carter administration has developed a bad habit of needlessly complicating its task as mediator. Last August, without consulting its Camp David partners, the administration announced its intention to sponsor a new UN resolution on Palestinian rights. When Begin and Sadat both objected, the President hastily retreated.

But in March, 1980, the Carter administration, courting Arab Middle East countries with single-mindlessness, managed to outdo itself.

After personal as well as telephone conversations between President Carter, Secretary of State Vance, and UN Ambassador Donald McHenry, the United States voted for a UN Security Council resolution that comprised a broad attack on Israel. Among other things, the resolution called for the dismantling of all Israeli settlements on the West Bank, including those established by Israeli governments preceding Begin's; it opened several cans of worms on the status of Jerusalem; and it undermined the "Camp David" peace process that provided for continued Egyptian-Israeli negotiations on the West Bank.

More than two days later, just before a meeting of the Israeli cabinet —and on the eve of a presidential primary in Massachusetts—Carter did an about-face and repudiated the vote—though it was never withdrawn. It was left to Vance to take the blame and give the unbelievable explanation that there was a "failure in communications"—but he then "re-avowed" the resolution!

The entire exercise resulted in angering both Israelis and Arabs. It also destroyed our credibility and lost respect for us among other nations.

This "mistake" was consistent with the administration's policy of applying continuing pressure on Israel, a friendly democracy, but one that did not happen to be blessed with oil.

Meanwhile, even before this action, unofficial delegations of U.S.

"And What Makes You Feel We're Not Being Even-Handed?"
3/2/79

pilgrims had gone forth for audiences with Yasser Arafat, head of the PLO. Vernon Jordan, president of the National Urban League, condemned these "flirtations with terrorist groups devoted to the extermination of Israel." Some of these American pilgrims were undoubtedly sincere and some unquestionably opportunistic. Some joined hands with Arafat to sing "We Shall Overcome." Who or what they and Arafat were going to overcome was not spelled out. But they said they wanted to bring peace.

What is often overlooked is the fact that the two major nations that were most deeply involved in four Middle East wars had already *made* their peace, however fragile it might be. And it was the most important peace that could be made in that part of the world.

More Arabs live in Egypt than in any other country, and it was Egypt that suffered the greatest Arab casualties. As one Egyptian writer put it, "richer Arabs want Egypt to starve alone, die alone, fight alone and go bankrupt alone."

Sadat's work for peace earned him the denunciation of most other Arab countries.

Israel, in return for recognition and peace with its greatest neighbor, was giving up by stages all Egyptian territory it held. This included pulling

New Marker
3/27/79

82

out all its settlements there, turning over airfields it had built and—probably hardest of all—giving up the oil fields in the Sinai that it had developed. It was banking heavily on a continuation of peace with Egypt —with Sadat and whoever might succeed him.

Israel also enjoyed at least one tangible gain: in April, 1979, for the first time since that state was founded, an Israeli freighter passed through the Suez Canal.

In 1980, when Russian troops moved to within 300 miles of the Persian Gulf, both Egypt and Israel offered to provide the United States with help in the form of bases, or whatever would be useful to us.

To the extent that Egypt and Israel began with a "separate peace," it is one we should have encouraged from the beginning. And if we are going to exert pressure, it should be on other leaders to follow the Sadat example of negotiation.

Our government is extremely conscious of the pressures on us that can be exerted by oil countries. It should also be conscious of the importance of having reliable allies. The Israeli democracy is one of the few reliable allies we have. And a stable, peaceful, and friendly Egypt is also important to us.

As for the costs to us of aiding these countries, we have spent far more elsewhere to gain far less. ■

**"Ah, We've Found The Man Who Can
Light The Way To A Better Day"**
9/19/79

**"He Was Busy On The Hot Line To
Vermont, Massachusetts, Illinois . . ."**
3/7/80

NOW, ON THESE CHARTS
OVER HERE . . .

I DON'T KNOW why I am constantly fascinated by televised weather reports. I'll sit through an entire local news program to get one. By the time it has come and gone, my ears are apparently so numb I don't know what I just heard.

Even the visuals don't help. I watch the satellite maps with clouds moving across them, and the radar maps with windshield-wiper circles running around them. These are animated versions of the unidentified gray blobs which Fred Allen used to throw on the screen in his North Pole lecture, when he would point to a murky area in one corner and explain solemnly, "Here is our base camp."

Instead of watching those weather maps around the world and across the country and trying to separate the local Fahrenheits from the Celsiuses, "solar indexes," and "dew points," I'd do better to stick my head out the door.

The economic news, especially out of Washington, is often just as foggy, confusing, and unpredictable, but it's delivered with a straight face and none of those jokes the weather reporters keep making.

The government economists, however, go through the same kind of explanations when their forecasts on inflation don't turn out right. They show, with charts, that we have the current inflation rate because food or fuel or housing or something else has gone up this month. If only it weren't for some combination of these things, we'd be all right.

The economic equivalent of sticking your head out the door to find out about the weather is setting foot in the neighborhood stores. For years, these indicated that inflation was blowing up a storm.

Unlike the weather, something could be done about it if we wanted to install wage-and-price controls. These had been renounced by President Nixon, who put them in place only as a surprise move before the 1972 election. The Nixon team, in the way it administered and withdrew controls, helped to give controls a bad name.

The Ford campaign to Whip Inflation Now was worth its weight in WIN buttons, which helped relieve the situation by giving everyone a good laugh.

President Carter expressed dismay at what he considered the lack of

"Now For My Next Trick—"
6/13/73

**"We Have A New Plan To Keep The Wolf
From The Door. We're Going To Call
It A Dog"**
8/1/74

"Remember, You Heard It Here First"
8/2/74

**"How Come We're Always Up In The
Front Lines?"**
10/2/74

"You Say You Feel Insecure—Lots Of People Feel Insecure"
12/4/74

"Now For The Bad News—"
1/8/75

The Lines
2/5/75

"Didn't You Used To Be In The State Department?"
4/11/75

confidence in the country shown by people who, with inflation running away with their paychecks, were not putting enough money into savings. In a reverse way, this matched the Depression effort of Herbert Hoover that urged people, through posters and ads, to engage in an "anti-hoarding" campaign—although most people didn't have any money to hoard and weren't sure how long their jobs or dwindling savings would last.

Money talks, and so does the lack of it.

A look in the stores, or a chat with the neighbors, would explain the futility of trying to get people to spend or to save, when their pocketbooks were doing all the talking they needed to hear. Government "jawboning" with business has not had uniformly good results, and jawboning with people about what they ought to do with their money is really a waste of time.

Jimmy Carter repeatedly insisted that he was against controls—though some commentators also insisted that in politics and economics nothing is certain.

Nixon's economic plans had "phases"—a popular term with government plans, which gives the impression that things are happening. Throughout the early 1970s, presidential plans for coping with eco-

Light Ahead
4/29/75

Ready For The Next Round
11/23/78

"It May Have A Lousy Rating But It's Looking Better All The Time"
8/24/78

nomic problems had more phases than you could find in a book on child-rearing.

Carter did not have phases but a succession of anti-inflation "programs." He even did a quick switch on budgets. In January, 1980, he submitted his annual budget to Congress. But six weeks later he changed his mind and sent up a different one.

"Guidelines" for wages and prices have been a more or less continuing feature of anti-inflation programs. These guidelines usually have a flexibility that permits them to bend or stretch to accommodate those who do not stay within them.

A longtime feature of the long-term fight against inflation—often described as our Number One Problem—was the failure to place sufficient emphasis on the energy situation. As long as we could not control energy prices, which were determined abroad, we could not control inflation at home. The oil-exporting countries, for their part, seemed surprised by inflation too. As their price increases triggered more worldwide inflation, they were amazed to find the dollars we paid them were worth less—so they felt a need to increase prices still more.

Both here and in the oil-producing countries, many leaders were like the people you read about in anthropology books, where the members of some obscure tribe have never quite figured out the relationship be-

1/13/78

"True, But This Month It's Largely Due To—
Ah, Yes, Here It Is—"
12/9/73

"It's A Whole New Design"
1/25/79

Bucket Brigade
4/24/79

"It Finally Arrived But It's Not Assembled"
10/26/78

"Betty, Remember All Those Jokes About My WIN Button?"
3/31/78

tween sexual intercourse and the birth of children. I tried to work up this idea into a cartoon sketch, but it didn't quite pan out.

Over a period of years there have been changes in our economics, which have become more cockeyed. Many of the predictions became good-news/bad-news jokes, in which seemingly good news was bad and vice versa. National productivity dropped, and we had "stagflation"—double-digit inflation booming along in a not-so-booming economy—often with high unemployment too.

By the end of the 1970s, things got so confusing that instead of the old line about prosperity being around the corner, some government economists (and politicians, who wanted the worst over before the 1980

"By Golly, It's Great How You Were Able To Get It Into
One Of Those Spaces"
4/13/79

"See Your Raise And Raise You Back"
8/29/79

"We've Got To Get Some Brakes For This Wagon"
1/13/80

"True, They're Somewhat Bent"
6/24/79

"Morning, Everybody—What's Up?"
2/11/79

elections) said rather hopefully that *recession* was just around the corner! They seemed disappointed that at the beginning of 1980 its arrival was still in doubt.

All this recalled a skit by some British comics who portrayed a group carrying signs declaring that THE END OF THE WORLD IS AT HAND. Their calculations have now shown them that today is the day and the moment is imminent. They greet each other with smiles and warm handshakes and chat enthusiastically as they check their watches. At the proper moment they look aloft for the ultimate catastrophe. As the sun continues to shine, and it becomes apparent that the earth will continue on its way, their smiles fade. When they look downcast and start to shuffle away, a member of the group says brightly, "Never mind, chaps. One of these days we'll have a winner." ∎

"This Chart Shows The Economic Pie—"
1/30/80

"We've Got A Complaint—This Stupid Money Of Yours Is Full Of Holes"
8/18/78

"I'll Give It To You Straight—You're In Trouble"
7/29/79

8/23/77

THE U.S. MARATHON

The U.S. Marathon
5/30/80

94

"Whew! I Was Afraid You Wouldn't Get Here"
5/1/80

THE RULING SERVANTS

PEOPLE IN PUBLIC LIFE used to talk about what a privilege it was to serve us. It still is, but in a different way. Over the years too many of them have been serving us less and enjoying more privileges for themselves. The downstairs has taken over the upstairs.

Hundreds of thousands of citizens come to Washington, D.C., each year and get a peek at their national government. Many arrive at National and Dulles airports. Those are good places for a first look at government privilege.

National terminal is so crowded that it is difficult to pick up or discharge passengers. It is a long way to carry luggage to and from a parking space, if you're lucky enough to find one.

In the midst of all this congestion and turmoil is a peaceful island of mostly empty parking spaces. They are part of a free area (closest to the terminal) reserved for members of Congress, diplomats, and Supreme Court justices—and sometimes used illegally by former congressmen and staff members as well. Some families of congressmen also park for days and weeks on end and pay nothing.

Why should *any* of these people have special free reserved parking at the airport?

But that is not all. Of 4,000 airport parking spaces which were "available to the public," 3,500 spaces were allocated by the Federal Aviation Administration to airport employees. The cost to each of the publicly and privately employed personnel who got these spaces was $15 a *year*. Moreover, some workers were allowed to buy two parking decals—the second at only $3 a year—because, as an official explained, "some people have two cars."

One of President Carter's most appealing promises as a campaigner in 1976 was his pledge to cut down the federal bureaucracy. A lot of voters hoped he would make many government agencies Bureaus of Missing Persons.

If the total number of employees did not diminish, at least Carter did try to curtail some government perquisites. He eliminated free parking for many executive department employees by instituting a modest plan that started with a nominal charge that over a period of years would increase to normal parking rates. But even this proposal (which did not take away precious parking spaces) brought loud protests from the professional representatives of government employees. They claimed that free parking was, in effect, part of a government worker's pay.

Privileges tend to perpetuate themselves. Officials who bestow them get to thinking they have a royal right to grant boons. And the recipients get to thinking they have a right to the privileges.

Many local governments have been belatedly concerned about a rip-off that has become routine. That is the abuse of disability retirements by police and firefighters. Even chiefs and deputy chiefs have been known to develop sudden disabilities shortly before leaving the service. These disabilities enable them to retire at increased pensions—generally tax-free—but do not prevent them from taking on second jobs that are at least as physically demanding.

When regulations have been tightened to prevent such generous non-deserved disability retirements, some employees acted as if *they* were being cheated. It was a rite which they had come to regard as a right.

Of federal workers, more than one in four retires each year on disability.

At the federal level, executive department and judicial prerogatives tend to get out of hand. Congressmen, who come to the capital as public representatives, also find that holding public office can be heady stuff.

"This Is Revolution! Next Thing They'll Want To Reduce Us To The Status Of The Common People"
10/31/79

"I Hear The Common People Have Problems With Something Called 'Social Security'"
5/30/78

Representative William Hungate of Missouri showed a great combination of humor and humility. When he decided to retire in 1976, he described what happens to a newly elected member of Congress.

The gist of what he said was that when you begin your duties, a staff member offers to shine your shoes, and you say, Oh, my goodness, no! A few days later a staff member shines your shoes and you don't object. A few weeks after that, you walk into the office, look around and demand: Well! *Who's going to shine my shoes today?*

The staff members, in turn, carry the pecking order on down and get to feeling that they are entitled to *their* privileges too. The citizen-taxpayer, who is supposed to be boss, sometimes becomes the ultimate shoe-shiner.

Congressional staffs keep increasing—even if the numbers of congressmen don't—and they become more visible in the workings of Congress. Staffers explain that the population keeps increasing and there are more constituents to serve. Constituent service is legitimate, but there is a point at which congressmen become like the old local bosses, getting re-elected by dispensing services and favors through increasingly large staff machines. Eventually, they could end up with a staff member for every few dozen constituents—like precinct workers.

In August, 1979, Senator William Proxmire made his monthly "Golden Fleece" award to the U.S. Congress itself. He said that in the previous ten years the House and Senate staffs had grown by 70 percent, from about 10,700 to 18,400, with cost of the staffs rising from $150 million to $550 million a year. "At one session of a recent congressional committee," he said, "some twenty-seven staff members were present to serve two members of the committee."

And the expanding staffs, of course, require more parking, more buildings, more restaurants, more space, more equipment, more money, more money, more money.

As the staffs increase, so do the office quarters. Congress long ago "outgrew" the Capitol building, and now occupies, in addition, three House Office buildings and two Senate Office buildings. In 1972, construction of a third Senate Office Building, to be known as the Hart Office Building, was approved—the cost to be $48 million. By 1979, estimates were $142.6 million and still rising. The congressional empire-builders showed no remorse for this profligacy. They maintained that if such buildings were put up immediately without question, we would save money on escalating costs because of inflation! How about a dozen more, fellows, before building costs go up again? A chance to get in on the ground floor, as you might say.

The east wing of the Capitol was rebuilt some years ago to provide more room in that building, and the congressional expansionists wanted to destroy the historic west front to provide another extension.

The extended new front would provide, among other things, more dining rooms, in addition to the ones Congress already has. How many dining rooms can a senator or representative and his guests eat in at one time? How much feeding space and recreational space is supposed to be provided for them or for staff members?

The members of Congress have their minimum-cost dining and entertainment facilities, which include *private* dining rooms. They also have saunas, gymnasiums, massage parlors, beauty parlor facilities, and swimming pools—not to mention hideaway offices for sharing a drink or whatnot.

In addition to special low-cost meals in the various dining rooms, there are cut-rate haircuts, free parking, and even free car washes in the House parking garages, paid for by—yup—the U.S. taxpayers. Then, of course, there are things like the health benefits at government hospitals, free trips that many get (first class) on military aircraft flights, and the junkets on commercial planes.

Some of their recreational facilities cannot be entered by reporters or photographers—no pictures or first-hand reporting for the public on the gym, the pool, the sauna.

I have a simple peasant view of such things. If congessmen have any recreational facility that we can't even see in photos, we shouldn't be paying for it, and they shouldn't be using it.

When their salaries went to $60,666.50 a year, many congressmen still

**"Here's My Latest Tax Cut Proposal—
Wait, I've Got It Right Here—"**
10/25/78

"He's Got It On Automatic Pilot"
2/18/77

complained about them. In addition to their salaries, they also get cost-of-living increases and pay raises that automatically take effect unless Congress rejects them. A familiar refrain is that they feel they have to maintain two homes—one in their district and one in Washington.

In all this housing talk, we seldom hear about all the built-in congressional back doors that augment their salaries. In 1979, the Senate repealed a proposal to limit members' honorariums to about $8,500 a year—leaving the limit on speaking fees at $25,000 a year.

Their large staffs—which we pay for—prepare a lot of those speeches for them. If a congressman should care to emulate Abe Lincoln and write his own speech on the back of an envelope, he has plenty of envelopes. We provide each congressman with a generous annual "stationery allowance" of several thousand dollars. He also gets no-cost long-distance phone calls and allowances for trips to his home district—which sometimes exceed the actual travel costs. In addition to the large amounts the government provides for staff salaries, congressmen receive an annual office allowance that comes to more than $80,000—apiece.

While the senators were voting themselves increased allowable outside income, the members of the House were trying to vote themselves another back-door increase—a tax deduction of about $14,000 annually for costs of living in Washington. This would have been in addition to the $3,000-a-year tax deduction they already allowed themselves for living in the capital.

It occurred to many observers that there was a way in which congressmen could automatically be spared all the hardships of living in Washington. They could retire.

It is hard to keep up with all the bargains. The National Park Service has provided the use of special guest houses for congressmen, their families and friends, at rates from $2 to $9 per person per day.

Although it is not part of their spending money, congressmen get franking privileges for their office mail, including "newsletters" to constituents, facilities for making radio and TV tapes to send back to local broadcasters, and other things to help them continue getting those congressional salaries they cry about.

Columnist Richard Cohen has written that more and more he finds himself muttering, "The hell it is." He wrote in 1979:

> The latest item to provoke my mutter was the explanation offered by William Whalen, director of National Parks, when asked why his employees were getting free tickets to the Wolf Trap Farm Park.
> "It's our park," said Whalen.
> "The hell it is," said Cohen.

A lot of other taxpayers also find themselves muttering more. The average guy doesn't necessarily think that government employees are all

"Exactly! We Need More Space"
5/26/77

101

wastrels and freeloaders. But, as Mr. Average tries to make ends meet, his spirits are not raised when he reads about annual government pay raises that keep government salaries ahead of his—plus "merit" raises that have nothing to do with merit. One government supervisor said, when interviewed about such everybody-up "merit" raises, "Since it is no one's money, you clearly like to be a nice guy."

The taxpayer's tensions are not relieved when he reads that the federal government spends over $1 billion a year on staff "training" programs, including one in which employees are given trips to Williamsburg, Virginia, for a week to "learn" to relax better.

The taxpayer's blood pressure is not lowered when he learns of officials playing numbers games to "keep down" the size of the federal bureaucracy. In one such game thousands of people are paid for fifty weeks of the year instead of fifty-two, so that they are not listed as full-time government employees.

The much larger numbers game is in what WDVM-TV reporter Bob Strickland has called "the Invisible Government." This consists of people employed on a contract basis, whose numbers are estimated as high as eight million. They are not listed on government payrolls and are often put on contract to avoid limits on hiring federal employees.

Among visible government employees listed under all kinds of euphemistic titles is an army of public relations people who act as press agents for their government employers and agencies.

Native Bearers
12/1/76

"All Part Of The Service When You Go With Us, Sir"
7/25/76

Government union leaders sometimes say that bureaucrats are "whipping boys" and that people in private industry also get whatever they can.

But there is an important difference: in most private industries, if company management and employee unions decide to jack up wages and prices and pass along the increases to the consumer, the consumer generally has an option. If such increases boost GM auto prices, he can make his old car last longer or buy a Toyota and say "To hell with GM."

But he cannot say "To hell with U.S."

The cost of government salaries and services is an area in which the consumer-taxpayer has no choice. He cannot bargain or refuse to buy. The governments (federal, state, and local) tell him how much to pay and when to pay it.

For this he should get the best possible service at the minimum cost, and with the fewest number of people on the payroll.

But he doesn't get that. And the costs don't stop with the current payrolls and benefits. They go on long after employment ceases.

In the pre-New Deal days of little job or retirement security, government employment involved a kind of trade-off. In return for fairly modest salaries there was almost total security and a pension. This was not a bad deal at a time when employees in private industry could be thrown out after years of work with nothing more than a pink slip.

Today there are many more government workers at all levels—federal, state, and local. Not only have their pay demands kept going up, but

7/2/78

Eruption
6/8/78

their benefits, including insurance and pensions, have gone up too. And that gets into very large figures.

Early in 1979, Congress found that the "unfunded liability" for federal pension systems came to $3.3 *trillion*. "Unfunded liability" is the amount of money pledged that the government has not financed.

Representative Gladys Spellman has counted sixty-nine retirement systems in which she says the government participates directly. Civilian government employees, incidentally, do not contribute to Social Security funds. They have much better pension deals, which most private business employees might envy. These have included cost-of-living increases every six months.

As for pension costs to the federal employee, the typical retiree gets back his total contribution within eighteen months of retirement. Long-service retirement at 80 percent of salary, plus semi-annual cost-of-living increases, gives some retirees more than they made in government.

Where government used to complain that it couldn't compete with private industry for good workers, some businesses are now complaining they can't compete with government pay and benefits—and some local governments complain that they can't keep up with federal pay scales.

In a *Washington Post* article early in 1979, Spencer Rich compared the pension benefits of hypothetical twins—one in private employment, the other in civil service. The government-employed twin works thirty

"You Folks Down There Are Going To Have To Row Harder"
4/18/79

"Same Here, Senator—I Don't Understand My Constituents' Worries About Health And Hospital Costs"
9/6/78

years for the government and can retire at fifty-five and begin drawing a pension—to which the government has paid most of the cost. He can then work in private industry for ten years, and at sixty-five he'll get a Social Security pension plus whatever pension plan the private industry provided.

The other brother retires at sixty-five, when he gets his Social Security plus private pension plan. With the identical life expectancy, the government twin collects over $319,000. The privately employed brother gets less than $170,000.

Military personnel can retire at a fairly early age, generally with a boost in rank just before retirement to lift the final salary on which the pension is paid. An officer might retire on a lifetime pension (with twice-a-year cost-of-living increases) and go on to a second career and a second pension. When that second career is also in government service, this is called double-dipping.

Perks also continue after retirement. Through government commissaries, an estimated 25 to 30 percent is saved on food costs by active and retired military personnel, now numbering more than eight million. About a quarter of these purchasers are estimated to be retirees, including colonels, generals, and admirals. Many of them already hold second jobs while living on lifetime military pensions.

Commissary privileges, like other perks, were established in times when government pay was low and government posts often far removed from grocery stores. By now the salaries are not so low, and the pensions are high, and the commissaries, subsidized by the government, are often near regular supermarts.

The higher we go in government, the higher the benefits.

Congressmen give themselves pensions, although they are supposed to be publicly employed from term to term and not on a permanent basis. But I probably shouldn't knock congressional pensions. In some cases voluntary retirement to get the pension is the only thing that can get them out of office at all.

The pensions run from $11,000 a year up. And in 1980 the members of the House of Representatives slipped themselves another little back-door payoff—a provision that present members of the House could, upon retirement, pocket any unspent campaign funds.

At higher levels of government, the per capita financial benefits after leaving office also come higher. Former speakers of the House not only receive pensions but going-away presents of money from Congress to ease their adjustment to private life, and in addition receive a former speaker's allowance of around $50,000 a year annually.

Officials who have been at the *very* top get top benefits.

U.S. News and World Report in 1979 tallied some of the costs to taxpayers of pensions, perks, and office help for former Presidents Nixon and

"I'm Feeling It Too, Buddy"
4/14/77

"I Can Explain Everything"
10/26/75

"We Seem To Be Accumulating Some Ice"
2/12/78

7/11/76

Ford, and found that their combined total was $800,000 a year. It reported that Nixon's tab included $163,329 for office and related expenses, $3,943 for long-distance phone calls, $3,569 for gasoline and other operating supplies, $540 for 200 photographs of himself, $35 for golf cart parts, and $480 for newspapers and magazines. Additionally, he got to keep some equipment used at San Clemente when he was in office—including "typewriters, couches, a refrigerator and five color TV sets." He also asked for increases for his travel allowance and to cover office expenses in 1980.

Ford's expenses for one year included $2,242 for plants in his office, and—of course—$100-a-month professional watering service.

Office plants? Watering service?

If we got rid of the Imperial Presidency, what are we doing with a Royal Ex-Presidency?

All the odds and ends of expenses for supplies, golf cart parts, staff, etc., are in addition, you understand, to their generous pensions, franking privileges, medical services, and other perks. These are on top of the large amounts they get for themselves through such things as books, lecture fees, TV interviews, and real estate deals.

Nor does all the $800,000 a year paid to these two men include the cost of the Secret Service protection they get for life.

There ought to be less secrecy about the Secret Service. We ought to know what chores they perform besides strictly protective ones.

When Nixon was President, the head of the Secret Service was involved in the installation of government-paid property improvements at San Clemente (including a new furnace) as being necessary for "security."

When President Carter moved to Washington, a news photo showed a Secret Service man helping Carter carry Amy's large doll house. That's nice. But you wonder how a sudden threat to the new President would be met by a guard who had his hands full of doll house. Several presidents used Secret Service agents as dog walkers, although there were no indications that the dogs were in mortal danger.

Former Supreme Court Justice Arthur Goldberg wrote in 1977 that the size of the Secret Service had reached staggering proportions and should be curtailed. He pointed out that agents were often used as nonprotective aides. He said they should "be relieved of acting as handymen" and that "a limited number of Secret Service personnel can provide basic security for the president and vice-president and their families." That would return its protective work to something like its necessary size and function.

The Secret Service, which is under the Treasury Department, was originally set up to prevent counterfeiting—a job in which it is still engaged. But it should not be a palace guard whose services can be offered as a privilege. Do ex-presidents need protection, or do they get Secret Service aides for life as a courtesy? Or to keep away autograph seekers? Or what?

Spiro T. Agnew continued to receive Secret Service protection after he was forced to resign—until there were complaints in Congress.

Spiro T. Agnew?

Some determination should be made as to what service of this kind should be provided for whom. After all, we're paying for those Secret Service people—along with all the other people on our government payrolls.

Economists of various political persuasions—and people with pocket calculators that can reach very large amounts—find that unless we change things, the escalating billions of dollars for civil and military government employees' pensions are eventually going to break the bank, and our backs along with it.

But there is something else. The notion that government employees are somehow *entitled* to special benefits, that public bureaus belong to the bureaucrats, that civil servants are entitled to be uncivil, that Congress can provide for itself whatever kind of facilities it wants and it's none

"On Those Letters About The Budget—
Tell Them We Are Thinking About
Money Matters Constantly"
4/4/79

1/16/79

of our damn business—things like that break the back of our democratic form of government.

Early in the century, Mayor Tom Johnson of Cleveland talked to Lincoln Steffens about the corruption of politics: "It's those who seek privileges who corrupt, it's those who possess privileges that defend our corrupt politics. Can't you see that?"

The millions of government employees in our country are not supposed to constitute a privileged class.

Having public servants who think the public is there to serve them—that's something we cannot afford at all. ∎

"What We Need Is A No-Frills Crew"
7/12/78

SCHOOL FOR SCANDALS

CORRUPTION, like Sandburg's fog, comes on little cat feet. It sits on silent haunches, but instead of moving on, it settles down and becomes bigger and more tigerish.

Once it's accepted that government people are privileged and that what they handle is "nobody's money," the privileges grow and the consciences shrink. Corruption becomes commonplace—a part of the government furniture, you might say. Furniture is a big part of government, and so are office supplies.

An Op-Ed piece in *The New York Times* by Tim James related the experience of a friend who was a summer employee of the U.S. Labor Department in Washington, D.C.

Shortly after the friend got there, a co-worker told him, "Now that you have your own desk, you can fix it up any way you want." She took him downstairs to the store run by the General Services Administration, which purchases government furniture and supplies. Here she helped him "refurnish his fully furnished desk," replacing every item to color-coordinate them. She even saw that he got an ashtray that he had no use for—all at GSA's expense. The "old furnishings" were then deposited in a closet already jammed with similar discards in good condition. The fledgling bureaucrat was appalled. Not only were the new office supplies unneeded and unwanted but no accounting was done for any of this GSA "shopping."

Little did he know that what he saw was only the frost on the tip of the iceberg.

A General Accounting Office auditor said he saw some $38,000 worth of new furniture stashed in a Department of Agriculture basement, and an attic bulging with it, much of it in unopened cartons. A floor of another building was filled with furniture from the Commerce Department—while it continued to order new furniture.

By GSA's own admission, it spends something over $200 million on new government furniture each year, even though there is no evidence it is needed.

From the Case of the Office Furnishings we now move to the Case of the Buried Furniture.

In September, 1979, it was discovered that the government was shipping furniture each day to a landfill near Washington at Lorton, Virginia, where it had been dumping furniture and office supplies for five years.

One owner of a surplus property store said he did well with material he either retrieved from the dump or paid the truck drivers to deliver to him. Tossed into the dump were working typewriters, adding machines, swivel chairs, files, cabinets, slightly used desks and bookcases—many of them of oak and mahogany. The surplus store owner said, "This thing really burns me up in a way. I mean, all the furniture does help me make a living, but damn, all the money they are wasting. It's our money, money they are taking out of my earnings. I guess I'm lucky. I get a little of it back."

After the newspaper stories began appearing, the dumping continued, but it became more difficult for anyone to retrieve anything. A truckload of furniture recorded as being from the Department of Health, Education and Welfare was dumped in front of a bulldozer with instructions to crush it immediately and bury it. The bulldozer operator tried to salvage some furniture for himself, "but they said, no way, that we had to get rid of the stuff right away." That could be called the moral equivalent of deep-sixing.

This might seem scandalous to you, but it didn't rate as a genuine scandal because it wasn't proven that anyone was directing all this for profit. Several government employees said that the reason usable property was thrown away was simply because it was easier to order new stuff than to move things or look into storage rooms. As one of them added, "Besides, people would rather have a shiny new desk than a used one anyway."

No big deal—nothing involved but the taxpayer's money.

The trouble is not that we have "faceless bureaucrats," but that to them we are "faceless taxpayers."

What's missing is the personal note. We need some kind of taxpayer-bureaucrat Big Buddy system, where each taxpayer will know which bureaucrat he's helping to support, and vice versa. We could keep in touch and ask, "What have you been doing lately?" "Are you planning to take off Thanksgiving week?" "Are the new office furnishings you got last month holding up all right?"

After a few articles in the paper about the furniture burying, the stories disappeared, along with the furniture.

But that might have been because they seemed small potatoes following the General Services Administration scandal that hit the front pages more than a year earlier. This did not involve furniture-burying; it concerned GSA's purchases of supplies and building maintenance for the government.

"We Did As Much As We Could In
Broad Daylight"
11/15/78

"I'll Have You Know, Sir, That I Am
Deeply Hurt By This Shabby Treatment
Of My Friend"
7/30/78

"Pikers!"
9/1/78

"I'm Not Some Cheap Looter Who Stole
A TV Set—I Sold Out For One"
10/24/78

In a series of 1978 stories by Ronald Kessler in *The Washington Post*, it was disclosed that the GSA, dealing in billions of dollars worth of purchases, was paying more for typewriters, calculators, cameras, video recorders, etc., than a private citizen would pay shopping for single purchases.

For example, GSA paid $612 each for typewriters available in retail stores for $541.

But the excessive payments on millions of dollars' worth of equipment were only the beginning. There were also billings for purchases never made at all.

And the purchases and non-purchases were only part of the scandal. Through GSA, the government paid for painting the walls of some buildings, in which the number of walls supposedly painted and repainted far exceeded the wall space in the entire buildings—buildings in which the walls sometimes were not painted at all. In addition to imaginary painting, there was imaginary maintenance work and payments to companies that did not exist.

The GSA scandal was complete with cash payoffs and kickbacks and bribes. With the estimated cost of the frauds running to more than $60 million a year, it has probably been the largest case of money corruption in American history.

Bringing this down to easier-to-grasp levels: in one case, four building maintenance contractors collected $580,000 from the GSA for repairs they never made on federal office buildings. Most of the money was used to bribe GSA building managers and assistant managers.

In another case, a contractor collected $1 million for phantom work.

In this huge scandal, a small feature was the mini-size payoffs to some people of mini-morality. In return for performing criminal acts—often certifying receipt of materials never delivered to the government—GSA employees testified to accepting for themselves a vacuum cleaner or some car tires, or a CB radio or a fireplace set.

There were also some mini-sentences. On swindles involving a $210,000 split with GSA employees and conspiracy with GSA employees to do the taxpayer out of a million dollars, U.S. District Judge Oliver Gasch fined two men $4,000 apiece—and required them to perform 200 hours of community service.

In another case, the same judge gave the same $5,000-fines-plus-community-service-hours to two contractors who had received $150,000 in GSA contracts for work which they admitted was worth only $120,000.

A former GSA employee who admitted taking $5,000 in bribes from contractors was fined $3,000 and sentenced to three years probation in Florida, where he was then living.

It doesn't take an electronic calculator to figure that when the size of the fine is less than the ill-gotten gains, white-collar crime often pays.

By May, 1980, the number of convictions and guilty pleas in the GSA scandals came to eighty-three—with more indictments likely.

Running along with the GSA scandals for a spell in November, 1978, were the "overtime pay" revelations. A congressional subcommittee found that the taxpayers were being ripped off on "overtime pay" by a number of government employees. Among these "overtime" cases, the subcommittee found that 600 federal employees received $7 million in overtime pay in a single year. This averages out to $11,666 of annual overtime pay per employee. One government employee showed that it was possible to receive a check from the government for an overtime request of $99,000 put in under the name of Donald Duck. In one instance, where only seven people were needed for overtime weekend work in a laundry room, twenty-one were assigned for "morale reasons."

The Department of Defense, which was spending some $400 million in overtime in 1978, could not tell a congressional committee how many employees were earning overtime or for what kind of work.

You might think these were scandals too, but they aroused less than overtime excitement.

In addition to scandals involving government employees, there have also been irregularities in government payments to the enormous numbers

"And Here Comes The Emperor In His Magic Robes, Followed By His Faithful Aides . . ."
5/25/76

"Uh—The Investigators Are Only Interested In Payments To Women, Aren't They?"
5/30/76

114

of consultants and others it pays on a contract basis. Some of these arrangements have involved conflicts of interest and illegal procedures.

Since 1974 we've heard persistent grumblings about a post-Watergate morality—implying that standards have somehow become stricter. They could hardly have been looser than they were from 1968 to 1974. But I don't think Watergate had the effect of tightening things up all that much. If anything, it left people numb about scandals. When you've had a president and a vice-president so corrupt they had to leave office, and many members of that administration who had to be sent to the jug, people have a hard time maintaining sustained outrage about scandals at lower levels.

The real reader-grabbers among scandals are the stories that literally have sex appeal. Congressmen are safer bedding down with special interests than with photogenic women. Everyone knew about Wayne Hays and the lady-friend employee who was not known for her typing ability. Everybody heard about Wilbur Mills and the show-biz lady who made the headlines with him. But there's something ironic about the fact that such men lost their committee chairmanships more because of these relationships than for their performances as chairmen.

Congress pats itself on the back for having made a small dent in the seniority system, but it still resists changing committee chairmen, how-

"Wait! Let Go—Not That Kind Of
Strip Routine"
12/3/74

"To Get The Most Attention, You Have
To Be Stacked The Right Way"
6/9/76

ever high-handed their operations or however low-level their private interests.

A prime example was Robert Sikes, who, as chairman of a House subcommittee on military construction, managed for years to use his position to provide boodle for his district and to find ways to enrich himself. But even after newspaper and television disclosures about him, it took all the courage his colleagues could muster to remove him from his chairmanship. House Speaker Thomas P. (Tip) O'Neill and Majority Leader Jim Wright hated to see him go.

The reluctance to oust chairmen for almost anything other than a front-page scandal hardly provides the best in leadership.

Congress worries from time to time about ethics. As the saying goes, it often wrestles with its conscience—and loses.

Both houses of Congress are reluctant to discipline their own members. This is partly because it's hard to sit in judgment on friends and colleagues—and partly for self-protection. If you raise hell about the other guy's ethics, who knows where the moving finger will point next?

In the Congress of 1978–79, sixteen-term Congressman Daniel Flood of Pennsylvania was indicted for bribery and conspiracy. After some plea-bargaining, Flood pleaded guilty to a misdemeanor and received a suspended sentence.

"How Could Anyone Think We're Not
Serious About Ethics?"
1/23/77

"Guess That Thrashing We Gave Him
Will Show Everybody We Mean Business"
7/30/76

116

Congressman Charles Diggs of Michigan was re-elected by the voters of his district in 1978 after being convicted of mail fraud and illegally diverting funds. In June 1980, when his court appeals failed, Diggs resigned.

Senator Herman Talmadge, who accepted money, gifts, and favors from Georgia constituents without bothering to keep track of any of it, protested that he was so busy being a senator, he didn't have time to be a bookkeeper. He was not too busy to sign vouchers for $43,435 in expense money falsely claimed for him. For his offenses the Senate demanded repayment of the $3,435 and $10,000 in unreported campaign contributions and found his conduct to be "reprehensible," tending to bring the Senate "into dishonor and disrepute." After dancing around the dictionary, it said he "is hereby denounced"—a word agreed upon instead of "censured." Senator Talmadge promptly hailed this as a victory and pressed on to run for re-election in 1980.

In February, 1980, the FBI made public its "Abscam" (for Arab Scam) operation. In this, agents who posed as rich Arabs allegedly induced a few congressmen to accept cash for services to be performed.

This disclosure did nothing to enhance the reputation of congressmen. It did not entirely enhance the FBI's reputation either, since the operation was leaked in advance via television before any congressmen were indicted or even accused of anything.

"Now To See Who Got Caught In What"
2/5/80

"After All, Our Camera Only Has One Eye"
2/8/80

Any congressman guilty in such an operation was doing something more blatant and more stupid than those obtaining "contributions" or "fees" for favors in ways only a little more subtle.

The Korean influence-buying scandal, which was not very subtle, was a big one which the government managed to kick around for nearly three years until it finally got lost.

From 1976 well into 1978, stories unfolded of the influence of the South Korean government on members of the United States government. A former Korean embassy aide testified that he had seen the Korean ambassador filling a briefcase with envelopes full of money for distribution on Capitol Hill. Several congressmen testified to having turned down envelopes of cash and gifts of jewelry and other valuables.

The best-known name in the scandal was Tongsun Park, a South Korean who had been known as a giver of lavish parties and a bestower of gifts and campaign contributions. Park left the United States in the fall of 1976. In August, 1977, he was indicted on charges of (among others) conspiracy, bribery, and failing to register as a foreign agent. In December, 1977, he was given immunity in exchange for testifying about influence-buying. In the spring of 1978, Park returned to testify before Congress. He told a Korean only-in-America "success story" of how he had risen from poor boy to rice dealer and wealthy man able to entertain prominent people in Washington and to lavish gifts on his friends.

"Your U.S. Senate Card—Don't Leave Home Without It"
5/31/78

Foreign Exchange
7/5/77

"What! Some Questionable Conduct At
This Finishing School? Tell Me All About
It So We Can Look Into It Together"
12/5/76

"When Do They Get To The Envelope
With The Names In It?"
10/27/77

8/30/77

"Gee, Dad, You Look As If You'd
Seen A Ghost"
11/12/76

But he refused to admit to acting on behalf of his government, and the South Korean government refused to send the former Ambassador, Dong Jo Kim, to the United States to testify. This must have been a relief to some congressmen because recipients of influence from foreign governments are subject to heavier penalties than recipients from people acting on their own.

In the end three sitting members of Congress were reprimanded.

The purchasing of influence in Congress is not considered an actual scandal when done by domestic organizations in the American Way.

Political Action Committees (PACs) are groups of contributors representing various interests. Between 1974 and 1979 by far the greatest increase in PACs was in corporations, which grew from 89 to 954. PACs contributions to members of the House and Senate, which were $12,500,000 in 1974, tripled in the next four years and continue on up.

When the House of Representatives, in October, 1979, voted a new limit on contributions by PACs, a check of the vote showed that members

"My, There Are A Lot Of Important People Here Tonight"
2/11/76

voting for the limitation received an average of $36,400 each, while those opposing it averaged $44,200 apiece.

Individual political contributors (who often identify themselves for the record simply as "businessman") contribute more heavily to incumbents than to challengers, and generally more heavily to Republican incumbents than to Democratic ones.

Incumbency is more important than political ideology. Willie Sutton, when asked why he robbed banks, said simply, "That's where the money is." The special-interest contributors have found that incumbency is where the congressional votes are.

Writer Jack Bass, who ran for Congress in 1978, told of soliciting a contribution from a "politically active vice-president of a major corporation." Bass says, "He was very direct: 'If you're an incumbent, we give $1,000 . . . and if you beat an incumbent, we give $1,000 to help retire your debt.' "

The large contributors expect something for their contributions. Years

**"The Trouble Is People Today Don't Seem To Have Faith
In Our Institutions"**
3/2/76

"Absolutely Gross!"
11/2/78

"I Came As Fast As I Could"
6/6/76

9/23/76

Incumbents
10/3/73

ago, a big operator complained about a politician, "We bought the son of a bitch, but he didn't stay bought." There are undoubtedly congressmen who accept contributions from groups but do not follow the wishes of those groups; but the odds would seem to be against biting the hands that fed their campaign coffers.

A tip-off on how all this affects government is that many of the heavy contributions are targeted to chairmen and members of committees involved with legislation of special interest to the special-interest groups. In late 1979, at least twelve of the twenty members of the Senate Finance Committee received money from contributors directly related to oil industries.

A further indication of how it all works is that a number of these "campaign contribut' ns" are made to incumbents who face no opposition. Such contributions leave little doubt about the relationship of the givers and receivers. It's the same when a congressman receives a fat fee to speak to some special-interest group—with the speech sometimes written by the lobby itself. Lobbies in Washington even arrange to schedule the speech while a congressman is on his lunch hour—a case of eat-and-run-to-the-bank.

There's a name for that kind of pay. It is followed by the word "off."

"Quitting Time And All's Well"
10/3/76

Meanwhile, the campaign contributions roll on. And Congress in 1979 continued to resist proposals which would involve public financing of campaigns.

Perhaps the biggest scandals in Congress are the ones in which it operates as a private mutual protection club. First there is the complacency with which congressmen accept unethical conduct—not to say corruption—by their fellow members. Second are the increased advantages of incumbency that congressmen give themselves—all the things they can do to ingratiate themselves to the voters—at taxpayer's expense. This in turn helps to produce the drift of heavy money toward those who already occupy the seats in Congress.

Those seats, like all that furniture handled by the General Services Administration, seem to have big price tags on them.

And what about that GSA? What has been happening there since the disclosures of its gigantic scandals?

Robert T. Griffin, who was assistant director of the GSA for years, was fired by the Carter administration. But the administration apparently had neglected to give advance notice to House Speaker Tip O'Neill—and since Mr. Griffin was a friend of Mr. O'Neill, this made Mr. O'Neill

Pre-Election Ballot Box
10/29/78

See How They Run
6/10/79

angry. A job was quickly found for Mr. Griffin on the White House Staff as Special Assistant to the Special Trade Representative at a salary of $50,000 a year—the same amount he received at the GSA.

Jay Solomon, who came in as the new head of the General Services Administration in May, 1977, worked vigorously to clean up the agency. He went out early in 1979—as the saying goes, "jumped, fell, or was pushed."

Solomon was replaced by Rear Admiral Rowland Freeman III. After a few months in office, Freeman transferred to a lesser job William A. Clinkscales, who had been an effective GSA director of investigations and assistant inspector general. Clinkscales had helped to start the investigations into GSA illegal activities that resulted in bringing many of the indictments.

As GSA administrator, Mr. Freeman was also in charge of the National Archives. His chief distinction in his new role was to announce to a stunned group of noted historians and archivists his plan to break up the archival records and disperse them to regional offices around the country. Admiral Freeman said of some records on Reconstruction, "They will go to Atlanta."

To the archivists and historians, Freeman's decision to scatter the records was as shocking as any scandal. But the more-than-self-assured Freeman told them, "I have a tremendous sense of history—I helped to make it . . . I'm an expert in almost every area you work." One Archives official said afterward, "Here's a guy who runs a housekeeping agency, who's in charge of the toilet paper, furniture, and cars, telling us how to run an archives. If it weren't so sad it would be funny."

What would also be funny, if it were not so sad, is that Admiral Freeman expressed the feeling that the GSA scandals were "overblown."

Six months after Admiral Freeman swivel-chaired into action, it turned out that GSA was still paying rent of $24,000 a month for a vacant office building in New York that was still unused.

Freeman also told an interviewer that he saw areas where the government could increase its private contracting that was already involving millions of people and billions of dollars.

When an auditor, conscious of past scandals, tested the GSA's payment system by having it issue checks to nonexistent companies, Freeman suggested that the auditor be fired.

As a further chill on auditors who uncovered waste and fraud, Freeman's deputy inspector general asked that they now be evaluated by their superiors on the basis of how well they develop "non-adversarial relationships" with GSA officials.

As more disclosures came to light, waste and scandals themselves were looking like government fixtures. ■

THE DARK AT THE END
OF THE TUNNEL

INDOCHINA IN OUR TIME has been tragedy without end. The American involvement in Vietnam turned poisonous and became divisive in the United States as well as in Indochina.

An indirect effect was the triumph of Richard Nixon over Hubert Humphrey in the 1968 presidential election. But the hope of peace, dangled before Americans in this election, was not to be fulfilled until after four more years.

There were four more years of Americans dying in Indochina, while scandals mounted at home. In withdrawing from Indochina, our government temporarily saved face and permanently lost lives—another 20,000 Americans.

Deceptions and casualties mounted together. Not only was there the

The Tunnel At The End Of The Tunnel
4/22/70

**"As I Get It, We're Going To Be
Vietnamized and Thai-ized, With A
Little U.S. Bomberizing"**
6/2/70

**"It Worked Fine—It Made Everyone Happy
To See Us Back In Vietnam"**
7/2/70

"You're Sure This Is The Way Out?"
2/9/71

"I Hope They Just Mean Civilians"
3/16/71

**"You Certainly Seem To Be Helping
SOME People To Help Themselves"**
11/19/71

"Now, As I Was Saying Four Years Ago—"
8/9/72

9/19/72

"Now They Tell Us"
9/26/72

11/30/72

secret bombing of Cambodia but there were falsified reports of missions, of casualties, of victories, and of losses.

Double casualties of the war were American veterans who came back from Vietnam. Unlike the veterans of other wars, most were not received with gratitude or acclaim, but with apathy and even suspicion.

Many Vietnamese who fled to the United States also found no welcome, although they too were often victims of our involvement in their country.

The cruelest of all tragedies occurred in Cambodia—a peaceful land that was to be blasted by bombs and torn by ground fire.

Cambodia had been ruled by Prince Sihanouk, a wily but thoroughly civilized man, who performed a diplomatic balancing act by making con-

Peace With Horror
1/11/73

Delayed-Action Bomb
8/12/73

Lasting Peace
1/29/74

"Maybe We Should Have Stayed There"
3/31/74

1/23/75

130

cessions to warring neighbors while maintaining peace within his country. In 1970, he was overthrown in a coup by Lon Nol, who ran a corrupt government.

Like a descent into the circles of an inferno, Cambodia went from the corruption and destruction under Lon Nol to the terror of his Khmer Rouge communist-government successor, Pol Pot. This madman uprooted or executed literally millions of his own people—perhaps a third of his country's population.

Even this was not the end.

Vietnam invaded Cambodia, bringing new terror, new casualties, hunger and disease, as Cambodians were ground between the merciless millstones of Pol Pot's forces and the Vietnamese. As one observer put it, the opposing forces were like a choice between cholera and cancer.

Cambodian ally China made "nose-bloodying" incursions into Vietnam. These incursions caused casualties on both sides without resolving anything.

The "boat people" of Vietnam, many driven out simply because they were of Chinese descent, were victims of another type of genocide. Their only hope was to seek refuge, if they could find it, in open boats. Refugees often gave up all their meager possessions to pay for the privilege of such an escape. Many died of exposure and disease in these overcrowded

"The End Of The Tunnel Is At Hand"
2/6/75

"If You Don't Bail It Out, You'll Be To Blame For Letting It Go Down"
2/26/75

3/27/75

Avalanche
4/1/75

Backfire
4/3/75

"Damn Americans! What Have You Done For Me Since The Last Eight Or Ten Years?"
4/22/75

and unseaworthy boats, which sometimes went down with all their suffering cargo.

In Cambodia, the survivors of the murders and the constant war now faced starvation. Often too weak to walk, they literally crawled on their hands and knees in efforts to reach the border of Thailand. Many could not make it. Some died within sight of the border. Those who got across were crammed into overcrowded camps, where flies swarmed around the drawn faces and twisted bodies of children dying from malnutrition.

Food aid was at first delayed by travel conditions in Cambodia and by an unwillingness of the United States government to deal with the Russian-backed Vietnamese aggressors. Later, aid to the Cambodians was withheld by Vietnam. The first priority was the troops. The killers always came first. Cambodians who had been hunted down and who had endured bombings and all the destruction of war were still losing their fight for life. Even when food got through, not enough medicine was reaching them.

Proposals for air drops of food and medicine had been regarded as impractical, not to say dangerous.

For the Cambodians, who never wanted war, the war went on. ■

4/2/75

"It Is Finished"
4/30/75

**"They Were Too Personal And Confidential
To Disclose, And Besides There Was
Nothing Confidential About Them"**
5/2/75

**"Some Of Them Must Wish We Had
Stayed Away From THEIR Towns"**
5/7/75

**"Think We'll Ever Get To The End Of
This Tunnel?"**
5/22/77

Cambodia Since 1970
1/10/79

The Lifeboat People
7/3/79

"Airdrops Of Food And Medicine? Do You Realize The Logistical And Diplomatic Problems?"
10/25/79

Ships That Pass In The Night
11/23/79

Year Of The Child
11/6/79

I BEG YOUR PARDON,
I NEVER PROMISED YOU . . .

REPUBLICAN CONGRESSMAN Gerald R. Ford, better known as Jerry, was a longtime party regular and a regular guy, who hoped some day to be majority leader of the House of Representatives. Nobody ever nominated Congressman Ford for president.

When scandal pushed Spiro T. Agnew from the vice-presidency in 1973, President Nixon tapped Ford for that position. And when Watergate drove Nixon from office the following year, there was Ford in the White House—the first president not elected to national office.

Ford came in with an enormous amount of goodwill. He described himself as "a Ford, not a Lincoln." To a nation weary and exhausted by scandals and national crises, that was good enough. He was giving the country a much-needed breather. Everyone was pulling for him.

That lasted for one month.

He then made the shattering announcement of the full, free, and absolute pardon of his predecessor.

This was given without receiving even an admission of wrongdoing.

Worse, it came shortly after Ford had given assurances that he would do nothing of the kind until seeing what the special prosecutor and the courts would do.

And, as if Nixon had left office in honor and glory, Ford asked Congress for a total of $850,000 for the ex-President—a sum so large that Congress wouldn't go for it. He also tried to give Nixon possession of the disputed tapes from his White House years and didn't succeed in that either.

Ford may have thought that the pardon would sweep everything behind him—and us. But it seemed more like sweeping everything under the rug. After all the shocks the nation had been through, this was just what it didn't need. It was also just what a new president didn't need.

The slate was not cleaned but smeared. The pardon was behind Ford, but it dogged him through his administration and his 1976 presidential campaign.

Likable fellow that Ford seemed to be, the public never gave him a full, free, and absolute pardon for that surprise announcement of September 8, 1974.

In October, 1974—more than a month after the pardon—President Ford made an unprecedented appearance before the House Judiciary Committee, which had voted the articles of impeachment against Nixon. Ford said he wanted to clear the record. As for any connection between his becoming President and his issuing the pardon, Ford declared vehemently that there had been no deal.

I have always felt that there was never anything written in blood. But, as Ford told the Judiciary Committee, he had been visited by President Nixon's aide, General Alexander Haig. Haig mentioned to Vice-President Ford half a dozen possible courses of action, three of which dealt with presidential pardons. One of these options specifically referred to a possible pardon of Nixon by his successor. Ford obviously did not then cry, "No deal." He asked Haig for details about presidential pardon powers.

In his efforts to put things aside, Ford sometimes seemed to follow a technique attributed to President Eisenhower. Ike told of how he dismissed from his mind people who angered him. He would write the offending person's name on a piece of paper, drop it into a drawer, and close the drawer.

What Ford did was to drop troublesome words from his vocabulary. At one point he decided to make no more references to Nixon—and

**"I'm Sure Glad To Know All This Was
For The Good Of The Country"**
10/20/74

"Ready?"
10/8/74

5/2/76

12/13/74

"Hey—It Reads Like One Of Them Presidential Pardons"
10/11/74

"Uh—I Guess You're Pretty Tired Of Bad News From Abroad—Right?"
4/6/75

didn't. Later he announced that he was dropping the word "détente."

The words and the problems they represented didn't go away, but they may have been gone as far as he was concerned.

Many other things, inherited from his predecessor, did not go away.

Ford, in the White House, was something like "Secondhand Rose," who never got a single thing new. Along with the office, and the cabinet, most of his problems were also hand-me-downs.

The recession that hit during his first year in office was not a Ford product. The energy crisis was not of his making either, and in trying to meet it, he imposed import fees, which stuck for a time. Many of his proposals were similar to those later advanced by President Jimmy Carter. Ford's program had the virtue of being presented when the crisis was at least a couple of years less acute.

The Indochina War was not a Ford product either. But it was during his administration that the war finally ground up the regime of General Nguyen Van Thieu.

In trying to keep things glued together in Vietnam, Ford asked Congress, in January, 1975, for an additional $300 million in military aid and offered more trips to Indochina for congressmen. But it was no sale. In the end, when people were clinging to helicopters during the

"He Was Taken From Us Before We Really Knew Him"
3/16/76

141

final days of our involvement, the enormous amount of military supplies left to the enemy did not indicate any shortage of matériel.

For a nation frustrated by failure in Indochina, Ford and Secretary of State Henry Kissinger provided action that was widely applauded at the time—the *Mayaguez* incident.

The *Mayaguez* was an American merchant ship, which was seized in May, 1975, by a Cambodian gunboat. Ford branded this an "act of piracy," demanded the release of the crew, and sent in Marines and Air Force helicopter crews. There was a costly landing on a wrong island, as well as other mistakes and accidents. Casualties among American servicemen came to forty-two dead and missing and fifty wounded. The number of dead was greater than the number of *Mayaguez* crewmen. (But in 1980, Ford pointed out that there were no other seizures of Americans during his administration.)

There was a good deal less vigor in another Ford–Kissinger decision a couple of months later. Ford pointedly refrained from seeing Alexander Solzhenitsyn, Nobel Prize author and famous Russian dissident, who came to the United States after being exiled from his native country. Ford's refusal to see Solzhenitsyn appeared to express fear of offending Russia.

At the end of 1975, Ford made a trip to China, Indonesia, the

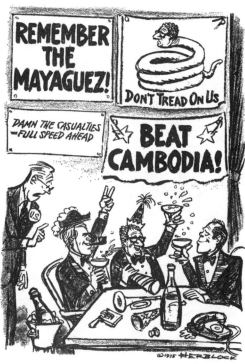

"You Sure You're Not Overdoing It
A Little?"
5/18/75

The Check
5/21/75

Philippines, and Hawaii. In Hawaii, he spoke of a "stable balance of power in the Pacific . . . partnership with Japan . . . normalization of relations with China . . . security of Southeast Asia . . . peace in Asia . . . cooperation reflecting the aspirations of all the people . . ." and a few other things. This was christened the Pacific Doctrine just before it was lost at sea and never heard from again.

A more important Ford trip took place early in his administration, when he met with Leonid Brezhnev in Vladivostok. Here they negotiated for a second strategic arms limitation treaty (SALT II). During the 1976 campaign, Ford was criticized by presidential challenger Jimmy Carter for not making better progress on SALT II. But it was Carter who later got bogged down in negotiating on SALT II, which then got bogged down in the Senate.

Ford also continued negotiations for a Panama Canal treaty. And candidate Carter asserted that if he were elected, he would never give up "complete control" or "practical control of the Panama Canal Zone."

During Carter's administration, negotiations for the Panama Canal treaties were concluded.

Ford's main problems were at home. Inflation reached a high of 6 percent before receding to less than 5 percent. This was a figure that by later standards might have deserved a "WIN" medal with oak leaf cluster.

Nevertheless, while Ford was president, the nation was hit with its

"It's All Right To Come Out Now. If You Had Met Him, Brezhnev Might Have Disapproved"
7/8/75

"Just Out Of Curiosity, How Did You Manage To Get Into It In The First Place?"
7/18/75

worst recession since World War II, with unemployment reaching as high as 9 percent.

Unemployment struck some top people in the Ford administration a year before the 1976 election, when he presided over a high-level shake-up, which included three cabinet positions and the directorship of the CIA.

At a press conference, when he was asked the reasons for the changes, Ford found himself saying over and over that "these are my guys—the ones I want."

One he most certainly wanted to keep was Secretary of State Henry Kissinger. And when Ford considered running for president again in 1980, he promised to bring Kissinger back with him—a second-time-around prospect that appealed to Kissinger, too.

There was one other pre-election casualty before 1976. When Ford became president, his nominee for vice-president was Nelson Rockefeller, who, after long Senate hearings, was confirmed. Later, in November, 1975, facing a nomination challenge from Ronald Reagan, Ford apparently decided that Rockefeller, who never sat well with the more conservative wing of the party, would be a liability. Longtime presidential aspirant Rockefeller voluntarily withdrew his name from consideration.

Ford was now ready for a spirited '76. ■

"Yours Looks Nice Too"
12/8/74

5/16/76

"Hear That Thump? We've Hit Bottom"
6/29/75

11/22/74

"They Can't Say I'm Not Doing Anything"
7/22/75

Easy Rider
10/1/76

SEE HOW THEY RUN

AMONG DEMOCRATIC COUNTRIES, our process for selecting a leader is the Steve Martin of political systems: a wild and crazy thing.

The founders did not envision the kind of political parties that later emerged. And those old-time parties did not foresee the individual approach in multiple primaries and caucuses, all taking place during and after nationwide polls that have fluctuated like yo-yos.

Nor did the old pols foresee the television commercials for candidates or the televised "debates," which are more like interviews by panelists. On election night we sometimes see on our screens almost instant projections of winners. These are preceded by indications of winners based on interviews with voters emerging from polling places that have not yet closed. The increasing press and broadcast coverage makes more hectic a political merry-go-round that is dizzying enough in itself.

Orange juice isn't just for breakfast any more, football is no longer only for autumn, and presidential campaigning isn't just for every fourth year now. It's for every year, every month, every day for breakfast, lunch, dinner, and supper. It is a political Endless Summer, with potential candidates and their staffs constantly searching for the right wave of public support.

The pause after elections is only a brief interlude to catch the breath before starting presidential preparations and speculations again.

The name of the game has become marathon. And the marathon men who run for president have the qualifications that used to distinguish successful filibusterers—endurance.

It is getting to be an endurance contest for all of us. The media and the mechanics of politics have taken over. In this game the candidates follow the Lombardi precept that winning is everything. More than that, they generally do so much talking about their techniques and strategy for winning that the voters may end up tired of trying to find the issues or to guess how a candidate might operate if he *should* win.

With notable exceptions, the most likely presidential nominees in the past have been current office-holders—governors, senators, vice-presidents or cabinet members. In 1976, Jimmy Carter was a successful candidate who devoted full time to running for president. After serving

"After They've Chewed Up A Few, You Get Your Pick Of What's Left"
3/4/80

"We Know It's Cockeyed, But It's The Only Roulette Wheel In Town"
2/24/80

Election Trends
11/17/78

one term as governor of Georgia, he spent the next couple of years running running running.

Four years later, others followed in his footsteps.

Senators such as Howard Baker and Robert Dole noted the disadvantage of serving in office while running against former office-holders who could give the campaign full time. Senator Dole said that if you want to run for president now, you have to be rich and unemployed. Former Governor Ronald Reagan and former Ambassador George Bush fit this description.

The big change in the system came with the vast increase in the number of states holding presidential primaries.

In 1960, when John F. Kennedy boldly ran for his party's presidential nomination via "the primary route," only fourteen states held presidential primaries, of which three or four were decisive. The nomination was not won until the party convention rendered its decision.

In 1980, the number of primaries totaled thirty-seven. This means not only lots of TV exposure and staffs working on image projection, but lots

"Well, So Much For The Eleventh Commandment"
3/5/76

of flying around, driving around, walking around, and shaking as many hands as possible. It also means spending more time plowing through the snows of New Hampshire.

Party caucuses in Iowa would be no big deal except that they come even before the first state primary—and Carter scored his first win there in 1976. So now the candidates, and the cameramen and reporters, tromp through the cornfields too.

One candidate who dropped out early in the 1980 race observed that "we live and die by an Iowa caucus." Just so. The early returns are like TV ratings, except that they don't even pretend to represent what the entire public wants. If a candidate doesn't score, his option is not likely to be picked up.

Some caucuses and primaries have little to do with determining actual convention delegates, but they count big in the "ratings" of the candidates' shows.

Political writer Mark Shields has observed that "the good old days" of smoke-filled rooms and proxy-filled caucuses really were not so good. But he has also pointed out the new problems created by the proliferation of primaries, campaign-spending regulations, and Democratic party attempts to base convention representation on a prescribed mix of men, women, various minorities, and "people who like their hamburgers well done."

Some reforms have functioned like wonderful new machines, which

**"Forward! We'll Head Him Off In
The Gulch"**
11/21/75

"Gee—A Medal From Gen. Goldwater"
7/2/76

need to be repaired by other new machines, which need to be serviced by still more new machines.

Shields has suggested one form of overhaul: regional primaries to be held the same day in several adjoining states. Others suggest a mix of same-day primaries held in scattered states within a "time zone" region.

However untypical of the country or however small their numbers, the voters in the early states have a more important voice in selecting presidential nominees than do voters in other states. Those later voters often don't get to vote for the candidates they'd like best because time and money have run out for the participants who don't score in the early races.

By mid-April, 1980, with many big primaries still in the offing, only two presidential candidates remained in each party.

If a lot of later voters want "none of the above," they may not be able to find an alternative because filing dates for primaries in many states are so early that it is difficult for some late entry to emerge. And

"Now We Turn On The Lights Again,
And—Hul-lo, What's This—Another?"
3/4/76

with more decision-making done before the convention, the prospects for dark horses are darker than ever.

After the conventions, voters dissatisfied with the major party nominees may have no serious alternative either. Many states require such early filings for third-party or independent candidates and have such a variety of complicated qualifying rules that it is difficult to place another candidate or national party on the ballot. And the federal-funds-for-candidates laws were written by major-party people for major-party candidates.

Among party primary candidates, the big word in recent years has been *momentum*, which George Bush referred to as Big Mo.

In 1976, my favorite presidential candidate was Arizona Congressman Morris (Mo) Udall, who was nosed out by Mo Mentum, under the name of Jimmy Carter. After the New Hampshire primary, it was Carter whose face blossomed on magazine covers and who was off and running ahead. Had there been one more or one less candidate in that New Hampshire race, Udall probably would have had the plurality and might have been followed by TV cameras for the next few months—or years.

The candidate who gets off to a running start is likely to keep getting attention and primary votes—and contributions.

In the 1976 primaries, problems with the campaign-funding law gave candidates added troubles. The matching funds they were to receive from the federal government were slow in coming at a crucial point. And

"That Guy On Roller Skates Somehow Spoils The Effect"
5/20/76

"But I Don't Think I Know Him"
6/10/76

**"When He Talks, You Can Tell He's
Using His Head"**
1/23/76

Sack Race
2/19/76

**"We Haven't Been Able To Assess The
Full Effect Yet"**
7/28/76

**"Cap'n, What You Need Aboard Is An
Albatross Expert"**
8/4/76

candidates who counted most heavily on those funds suffered from the delay.

The Carter 1976 campaign was a media model, in which the candidate showed early the importance of symbolism. He was frequently photographed carrying a suit bag over his shoulder during his travels—just a common man with a political retinue that could have carried all his bags all over the country.

Carter pressed on, pressing hands. In the roller-coaster political style that has since become identified with him, he lost some later primaries —and momentum—but made it to the convention and the nomination. For second place on the ticket, he selected Senator Walter F. Mondale, who was an asset in the election.

A word is in order about the two major parties. The Democrats often engage in donnybrooks but usually pull themselves together—or pull in enough independent voters to do pretty well at election time.

The Republicans have generally been divided between those who regard the party as a private club with strict tests for nominees and those who want to give it a broader appeal.

An example was the struggle for the 1952 nomination between Senator

"That's Carrying The Nostalgia Craze Too Far"
5/4/76

"You're All Set—As Soon As That Heals
You'll Be Right Back In Critical Condition"
8/19/76

"Let's Go Over It Again—Say He Mentions
Nixon. You Look Puzzled And Ask, 'Who?' "
8/22/76

"During The Debates He Wants To Keep
Up With His Work"
9/21/76

"Not Free? I Can't Get Over It! There
Was Dancing In The Streets"
10/10/76

Robert A. Taft (Mr. Republican) and General Dwight D. Eisenhower. After a hard tussle, the nomination went to Eisenhower, who was one of the most popular men ever in public life. The closed-club wing of the party may have taken some solace in the fact that on some domestic policies, Ike turned out to be more conservative than Taft.

President Gerald Ford got to the White House without being elected to it, but he had a rough go in 1976 trying to win a four-year lease on it. Ronald Reagan, his principal opponent for the nomination, gave him a real-life let's-win-it-for-the-Gipper nip-and-tuck fight all the way. He may also have pushed Ford into more conservative positions than Ford would have liked.

Right down to the 1976 Republican convention, the race was so close that uncommitted delegates and even alternates found themselves being treated like royalty as the opposing candidates wooed them.

In the hectic pre-nomination jockeying, Ronald Reagan made a radical departure for a candidate. He announced in advance the name of his potential running mate—Senator Richard Schweiker of Pennsylvania, who was regarded by many Republicans as too "liberal." It was a political "calculated risk."

Ford just managed to eke out the nomination. To replace his vice-president Nelson Rockefeller, he chose as his running mate Senator Robert Dole of Kansas, who was more conservative and abrasive.

"... And If I May Be Allowed A Moment
For Rebuttal ..."
9/24/76

"Ford Is Rocked By A Left To The Jaw—
Carter Takes A Hard Right To The Mouth
—Both Men Are Hurting—"
10/13/76

"You Ain't Pledging Your Loyalty To The Godfather?"
11/27/77

"You Just Think Lovely, Wonderful Thoughts And They Lift You Up In The Air"
—*Peter Pan*
8/8/79

"Rosalynn, It's Him Again"
9/12/79

"But He's Very Good In Political Races"
11/9/79

The political assets of a White House incumbent are never to be underestimated. In the 1976 election contest with Carter, Ford literally used a "Rose Garden" strategy—signing bills there, with the White House as a background.

Incumbents seldom debate their opponents, but with Carter running ahead in the polls, Ford engaged in a series of debates with him. These followed the pattern of the Kennedy–Nixon debates of 1960, in which the candidates made opening and closing statements and answered questions put to them by a panel.

Anything can happen in an election—or a "debate." They can be lost in strange ways and in foreign places.

In 1960, if Richard Nixon did not lose the election in his makeup room, he may have lost it in a place John F. Kennedy kept emphasizing was only ninety miles from our shores—Cuba.

Ford may have lost the 1976 election, or at least the "debates," in Poland. That was the country he said—in one of the debates—was not under Russian domination.

Carter discovered that in presidential campaigns, little things can mean a lot. During the 1976 campaign an interview with him—containing an observation on lust—appeared in *Playboy*. The magazine issue was more talked about than most political issues.

In another interview he used a phrase that caused him trouble.

"Are We Angry Enough To Want Somebody Who Really Means Business?"
11/16/79

12/5/79

157

"We Shall Fight In The Speeches, We Shall Fight On The Flagpoles, We Shall Fight On The Bumper Stickers . . ."
1/11/80

"Never Mind That Matching-Funds Stuff —How Much Is It?"
12/13/79

"Talk About Inflation!"
2/27/80

"I Just Happen To Have Found This Free Time Just Before The Iowa Caucus"
1/17/80

Possibly in an attempt to compete against Nixon–Ford administration appeals to voters who opposed desegregation, Carter mentioned the desirability of neighborhoods retaining their "ethnic purity." This phrase later underwent some purification when he explained that it wasn't meant the way it sounded.

While the White House provides a built-in advantage for an incumbent presidential candidate, there is also a campaign advantage enjoyed by the non-incumbent.

He can promise everything the incumbent is not providing. He can offer hope to everyone who wants things done differently.

In the '76 campaign, Carter promised that he would never mislead people. He also gave the impression that he would bring down inflation (then raging at 4.8 percent). In the fourth year of the Carter administration, inflation hit an annual rate of 18 percent. In 1976, before he was elected, Carter was also going to bring down interest rates, reduce defense spending, and a number of other things—and you could depend on it.

There has never been a candidate or a president as consistently upsy-downsy in the polls as Jimmy Carter. After building an apparently sizable lead over Ford in 1976, he almost managed to blow it, but won by a narrow margin.

2/15/80

"He Can't Campaign Now—He's Up To
His Ears In Crucial Re-Election Politics"
2/13/80

With Carter's election, the presidential campaign of 1976 was over—and the campaign of 1980 could begin.

First-term presidents are inclined to think about second terms—and Jimmy Carter was certainly no exception. Presidential and vice-presidential hopefuls who missed out the last time think about running again. And with the early starts needed these days, they start thinking early.

Ronald Reagan kept right on running.

John Connally still wanted to run.

Senators Robert Dole and Howard Baker had tried hard for Number Two spots and were ready to try harder to be Number One.

California Governor Jerry Brown, who had won some late primaries in 1976, simply kept on running.

And former President Ford, announcing that Reagan was unelectable, said he was ready to answer a call from his party. A short time later, after consulting with his advisers, he declared his non-candidacy.

A refreshing new face in the Republican contest was Congressman

"Well, Hello!"
3/6/80

John Anderson of Illinois, whose ideas and outspokenness made him a standout.

But the big new starter in the 1980 campaign was Senator Edward M. Kennedy of Massachusetts, long talked of as a possible Democratic candidate. And the biggest political surprise was the way Kennedy and Carter quickly changed places in the polls.

Prior to Kennedy's announcement, surveys showed him running far ahead of Carter, who registered his lowest rating yet. The saying was that the nomination was Kennedy's for the asking.

But when Kennedy finally asked, he got a cool response in early polls and primaries. This was partly due to his apparent lack of preparation for a real contest. But it was also largely due to events outside the country.

The seizure of the American embassy in Iran and the prolonged holding of Americans as hostages there made the President the flag to which the nation rallied. Carter shot up in the polls and Kennedy plummeted.

Month after month, Carter kept talking about his concern for the hostages. Remembering the hostages became as good as remembering the *Maine* or the Alamo.

"Life," as President John F. Kennedy had said, "is unfair." That same

"Not Quite The Slogan We've Been
Looking For"
4/18/80

"So This Guy Rocky Wins Another Round
—You're Still Way Ahead On Points"
4/24/80

President had noted with wry amusement that after the Bay of Pigs fiasco, his own popularity had risen. He remarked that the worse he did, the better he came out in the popularity ratings.

But that's the way the polls bounce.

After he began leading Senator Edward Kennedy in the polls, Carter canceled out on a debate they were to have had. The excuse was that he could not go out on "the campaign trail" until after "the hostages are back here, free and at home." But the hostages had been seized and held before he agreed to the debates. All that had changed was his political standing.

Another foreign event also gave him a boost. When Russia invaded Afghanistan, the tanks rumbling into that poor country were, for 1980 political theater, a veritable *deus ex machina*.

In a column aptly titled "The Make-Believe Memo," Richard Reeves wrote of a purported private memo to Carter from his longtime confidant and press aide Jody Powell. It gave reasons why Carter *should* debate Kennedy before the Iowa caucus—but oddly enough, it listed no reason why it was advantageous for Carter to *avoid* the debate. He didn't even give the President an option. At the bottom of this "private memo," soon to be leaked to the press, Carter formally wrote to his longtime friend, "I can't disagree with any of this, but I can't break away from my duties here, which are extraordinary now, and which only I can fulfill. We will

"We'll See What Those Stupid Voters Have Given Us This Time"
11/3/78

"Here's The Strategy—You Have Your Name Legally Changed To 'Neither-Of-The-Above' . . ."
4/9/80

just have to take the adverse political consequences and make the best of it. Right now both Iran and Afghanistan look bad and will need my constant attention."

Political observers noted that Carter apparently had time to make plenty of political phone calls to states where primaries were being held, and to appear on TV just before primaries with announcements of hopeful international developments—that later failed to work out. With all his duties he even managed to appear (following a primary setback) at a political fund-raising dinner. And while talking of budget belt-tightening, Carter poured federal funds into states and cities where he needed votes to win the nomination.

In 1980, it was incumbent Carter who was accused of hiding in the Rose Garden. But it would be more accurate to say that he was hiding behind the flag in the Oval Office. _n this campaign he was not above accusing other presidential aspirants who criticized his policies of "injuring the national interest" and helping the Russians and the Iranians.

After the failure of the rescue mission to Iran, Carter announced that

"If God Meant For Us To Fly, He Wouldn't Have Given Us Donkeys And Elephants"
4/25/80

4/29/80

the crises were now "manageable" and he could campaign away from the White House.

No matter that events abroad might have been prevented or were bungled. The polls and primaries early in 1980 showed Carter running well in his all-out quest for renomination and re-election.

Old movie houses and theaters used to run the cautionary line: "Program subject to change without notice." The same can be said for the political theater.

One poll—probably as accurate as any—was taken after a couple of 1980 New England primaries. It indicated that many people didn't make a final decision until they reached the voting booth.

That explains the changes that can occur during a presidential campaign—where the polls giveth, the polls taketh away, and sometimes the polls giveth back.

But it doesn't explain how we can so often get down to final choices that are unsatisfactory.

In the spring of 1980 voters who were depressed by what seemed a probable November contest between Carter and Reagan looked forward to having another choice. John Anderson, who recognized that he could

"With These Rosy Glasses, I Don't Have To
Do All My Campaigning From The Garden"
5/4/80

"It's Not As If It Were Something Important
Like A Political Campaign Event"
5/9/80

"You Call That A Choice?"
5/23/80

not win the Republican nomination, withdrew from that race and announced his intention to run for president as an independent.

Longtime White House correspondent Edward T. Folliard used to say that there was one ingredient necessary for every presidential candidate —luck. And he was right.

But the voters shouldn't have to depend on it so much.

Our process for nominating candidates for president and vice-president still needs to answer the question mentioned by somebody before the 1976 campaign: Why not the best? ■

5/29/80

"That Last Overhaul Needs An Overhaul"
11/5/76

VISITOR TO WASHINGTON

AFTER FRANKLIN ROOSEVELT began his first term as president, he found that he was going to have to adopt programs that cost lots of money. But during his campaign he had given a stirring speech in Pittsburgh, in which he denounced government spending and "loose fiscal policies." He mentioned this to his adviser Sam Rosenman and asked how the difference could be reconciled. Rosenman replied, "Deny you were ever in Pittsburgh."

In 1976, Jimmy Carter campaigned for president as an outsider—a non-Washington or anti-Washington candidate. As he prepared for his 1980 re-election campaign, with many earlier promises unfulfilled, it looked for a while as if he might deny he was ever in Washington.

In late July, 1979, he was speaking publicly about Washington as an

"And Now, For Those Who Want A President With No Experience In Washington—A Man Who Never Even Heard Of Washington!"
2/29/76

This Time It Vanished Quite Slowly, Beginning With The End Of The Tail, And Ending With The Grin
—*Alice in Wonderland*
5/10/77

"Could You Hold It A Minute? The
Patient Seems To Have Acrophobia"
4/29/77

"If They Think The Canal Is Tough, Wait
Till They Try Coming Up The Potomac"
5/19/77

"isolated world," an "island" where he had supposedly been running
the government for two and a half years—and where he wanted to be
sentenced for another term.

Although I don't go in much for election predictions, I did make a
kind of *post*-election one about Carter in 1976. This was to a colleague
who said that candidate Carter had been very fuzzy, but that President
Carter would soon have to make decisions, reconcile discrepancies, and
come through more clearly. I told him I thought that Carter might go
through an entire term in office and run for re-election still being fuzzy,
and without people quite knowing what he was like.

Emerson may have been right about consistency being the hobgoblin
of little minds, and most of us don't want in the White House an ideologue
who carries everything to an illogical conclusion. But Carter managed
to be consistently inconsistent and firmly vague.

As Lucy said to Charlie Brown in Charles Schulz's strip, "If you're
going to be wishy-washy, be definite about it!"

When parts of a Carter program were not passed, Congress was to
blame. At the same time, he could assure press conference questioners
that Congress was doing very well, and they were getting along just fine.

"It Comes Out Fuzzy"
5/21/78

Carter could engage in straight-faced low-key hyperbole that was flexible to the point of snapping the imagination. Anything could be the greatest or most dangerous or most important. And almost any other politician with whom he appeared was his greatest friend and the finest public servant in the history of the city, state, or nation.

In legislative proposals, Carter could also be flexible. One of the hallmarks of his administration was the "movable centerpiece." In every plan there was what he called the centerpiece of his entire program. When that centerpiece went down, he pointed to some other section as the centerpiece.

In addition to the movable centerpiece, there was also the movable rug, on which he and his supporters in Congress could take a stand for something he said was most important. Then, without advance notice, he might disappear, taking the rug along with him and leaving the congressmen in mid-air.

A foreign ally could also find himself treading air if—for example—he publicly agreed to an American request to install neutron weapons in his country, only to find later that Carter had decided to abandon them.

When Carter and his political advisers apparently decided that he needed a tougher image or a tighter inner circle before going into the

4/15/77

"It's The Cartron Bomb—It Knocks Down
Supporters Without Damaging Opponents"
4/7/78

"Brother Jimmy Has Been Losing Altitude"
9/13/77

"I Still Say It Doesn't <u>Look</u> Right"
8/10/77

**"That's Strange—According To Our Map
We Should Be At Mount Confidence"**
1/27/78

"That's Making 'Em Roll, Ham"
7/20/79

1979–80 presidential campaign, some of his cabinet members suddenly found their heads in mid-air.

Later in 1979, Carter publicly lamented the fact that political campaigns now started so early and ran on so long. He seemed to have forgotten that it was he who set a new record in time spent running for the office.

Carter continued to place heavy emphasis on symbolism—the symbolism sometimes seeming to be more important than policy. Many will recall Carter appearing in a sweater for a TV speech on voluntary measures to cope with the energy crisis. The sweater wore better than the speech—or the thermostat controls he spoke of.

In a 1979 "non-political" campaign trip, Carter took a train from Washington to Baltimore. The trip gave him a chance to talk about energy conservation and express an interest in trains, even though the administration had already cut back train routes and schedules.

Many of Carter's energy speeches were so non-energizing that listeners felt he was talking about a crisizzzzzzzzzzzzz. In an attempt to

"It's The Political Gong Show"
2/13/79

"Look—Maybe Up Ahead There"
4/26/77

"That Was A Very Good Vault—Now,
Lower The Bar For My Next One"
1/25/78

"Hey, Man, I Hear They Might Send An
Exploratory Delegation To Darkest
Innercity"
9/1/77

"We Can Say, Then, That's He's Doing
Fine Except In Two Areas"
4/4/78

punch up a speech, he made a fist for the camera and brought it down on the desk. This was in the delayed speech of July 15, 1979, in which he seemed to blame the country for *its* failure to assert leadership.

After announcing a presidential energy speech was upcoming, the White House postponed it, and the President went to Camp David for ten days, ostensibly to work on a new speech. Each day, the TV screens showed groups of public and private citizens—congressmen, business and labor representatives, "teachers and preachers"—being helicoptered to Camp David to confer with him. When sufficient interest was built up, Carter went on television to let the country know that it was suffering a malaise—a "crisis of confidence," a "crisis of the American spirit" that apparently went back to Vietnam and Watergate.

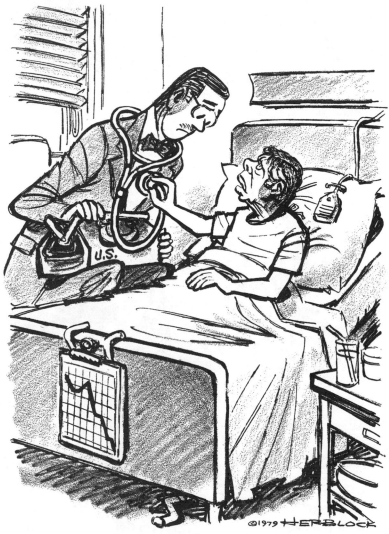

"I Think I've Diagnosed Your Problem"
7/17/79

"So Long, Fellows—This Is Where I Get Off"
8/25/78

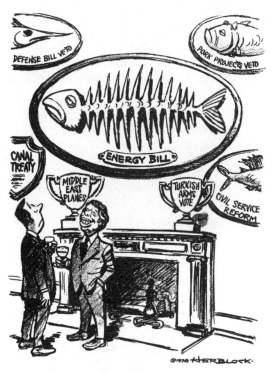

Trophy Room
10/12/78

"And Now, In This Hat—"
3/20/79

**"I'm Going To Give It To You Straight—
I Don't Have Any Idea What I'm Doing"**
4/27/79

At the beginning of his 1975 campaign book, *Why Not the Best?* (which he said was *not* a political autobiography) Carter wrote:

> The tragedies of Cambodia and Vietnam—the shock, embarrassment and shame of Watergate—the doubt and confusion surrounding the economic woes of our nation have created unprecedented doubt and soul-searching among our people.

A couple of pages later he concluded that among the American people "there is a willingness and even eagerness to restore in our country what has been lost—*if* we have understandable purposes and goals and a modicum of bold and inspired leadership."

Judging from his 1979 speech on our malaise as a nation, his administration had not provided that modicum of bold and inspired leadership. Only, it seems, that was not his fault. It was ours.

In 1979, running far behind in the polls, Carter found that it was his countrymen who were lacking. These were the same people that he had

"Who's In Charge Here?"
7/18/79

referred to in his campaign when he promised a government as good, as decent, as compassionate, as filled with love, etc., as they were. Later, when Carter picked up in the polls, he apparently found the nation to be pulling out of its malaise.

It was in that July, 1979, energy speech that Carter delivered the Nixonesque advice: "Whenever you have a chance, say something good about our country."

About half a year after Carter's early 1977 speech on "the moral equivalent of war," I wrote an imaginary speech on how he might have coped with an earlier and greater emergency. Since he had been in office less than a year, it might have seemed a little tough. Looking at it now, it seems to be a fair enough take-off on the Carter style during his first years in the White House:

THE MORAL EQUIVALENT OF ENERGY
Address by President Carter
December 20, 1941

Many of you have heard by now of the unfortunate bombing of Pearl Harbor that took place on December 7, a date that will live in many memories as a sad one.

I had planned to speak to you nearly two weeks ago but rescheduled this broadcast to provide time to prepare a program and to have further meetings—involving extremely delicate negotiations—with representatives of the Imperial Japanese government who are still in this country.

Our talks, which have been useful and hopeful, have covered a wide range, including the need for a Japanese military homeland in Hawaii, and our need for repairs at Pearl Harbor and to our vessels there. We intend also to ask that they consider, as a matter of urgent priority, the return to us of the Philippines, Southern California, and Oregon.

These are matters of concern to all of us, even if we do not live in Pearl Harbor or the Philippines or Southern California or Oregon. The loss of these areas could have serious consequences for our people as well as for our friendly relations with the Imperial Japanese government.

If there is no improvement in these relations, we will be faced with a very serious situation, and I am asking Congress for legislation to deal with the major problems confronting us. This legislation, which we have planned carefully, will call for sacrifices on your part to meet the emergency.

Our program is divided into three main sections. The first of these concerns Japanese toys. In recent years, we have imported millions of dollars' worth of toys from Japan, imports that have steadily risen. Each of us—and the children and grandchildren in our families, which form such a basic unit in our country—must learn to make do a little longer with the Japanese toys we already have, instead of importing newer and greater numbers of Japanese toys every year. This will be a hardship for some, but it is necessary, and I am meeting with leaders of both parties of Congress next week to ask if their families will go along with this measure.

The second part of our program is of even greater importance and affects still more of us. This involves tea. Our country is less dependent on tea than some others. Nevertheless we have been a tea-importing country, and much of our tea comes from Asia. A reasonable cutback in the consumption of tea should help during the present emergency, without working undue hardship on the importers of tea or manufacturers of teapots and tea tables in our country. I shall consult shortly with members of Congress, who may have tea shops in their districts, to ask what they consider a fair and equitable tea program.

As substitutes for tea, there are several alternatives. Our own Coca-Cola is a popular beverage, especially in my native Georgia, though it is seldom served hot. Milk is a nutritious and versatile drink, which can be served hot in cocoa or can be used cold on our native American corn flakes—what the Indians used to call maize. Milk has the advantage that it can also be made into cottage cheese. This can be served with root beer, another moral equivalent of tea.

The third part of our emergency program concerns travel abroad. Many of you have probably looked forward to a vacation in Hawaii or the Philippines. I have postponed my own plans for a trip that was to include stops at Tokyo, Peking, Manila, Brazil, Outer Mongolia, the Canary Islands, Tierra del Fuego, and Yonkers.

We must face the fact that we may not be able to vacation in Hawaii or the Philippines this winter, or perhaps for several winters. I shall ask that you travel instead to places like Miami Beach, Las Vegas, or Acapulco. Such changes also will involve sacrifice, but in the present emergency there is no other possible way. I shall meet soon with members of the Congress and with representatives of American travel bureaus to ask if they know of any other way.

These three groupings—toys, tea, and travel—provide the carefully integrated plan we have worked out to deal with the present Pearl Harbor emergency. If any sections of this plan are not approved by the Congress, we will try to replace them with other parts, providing the replacement parts are not imported from Japan.

The sacrifices involved in this emergency program will be a test of our national will and character and strength, our mercy and mildness, our forbearance, decency, honesty, consideration, and goodness, our willingness to love, honor, and cherish, in sickness and in health, our desire to be trustworthy, loyal, helpful, friendly, courteous, kind, obedient, cheerful, thrifty, brave, clean, and reverent, and our capacity for national survival and all-round good sportsmanship.

To succeed in this national test it is absolutely crucial that we achieve *all* of our objectives—or most of them—or perhaps some of them. And if we do nothing at all, at least we will know that we have done our very best.

Thank you. ∎

"Don't Let Other People Hand You
Any Baloney"
5/2/79

"It's Such A Big Success We Want To
Build Another One Over Here"
6/5/79

"You See, The President Didn't Create
This Crisis, And He Feels Sure That If
The Government Is Prudent, Private
Enterprise Will Eventually . . ."
6/28/79

7/24/79

"This Is Fun—What Do I Get To Play Next?"
8/16/79

"You See, Kennedy Would Spend More On Social Programs Than I Would"
10/24/79

"Well, Let's See What Our Domestic And Foreign Policies Will Be Today"
4/22/80

2/29/80

Energy Policy
5/28/76

THE LETHARGY CRISIS

IN GILBERT AND SULLIVAN'S *Pirates of Penzance* there is a scene in which a general sends the police force to do battle with the pirates. The policemen sing—with a "Tarantara!" here and there—"We go!" They keep singing "We go! . . . Yes, forward on the foe!" until the general observes, "Yes, but you *don't* go!"

Throughout the 1970s we heard from three administrations that they were off to fight the energy problem and to end the piracy of the international oil cartel.

As they trumpeted "Tarantara!" with varying degrees of certainty and uncertainty, oil prices shot up, inflation rose, and oil imports increased. The oil-exporting nations tightened their grip on the American economy and increased their influence on American foreign policy.

One of the most direct means of curbing overdependence on oil imports is to impose quotas or tariffs. More than twenty years ago we *had* quotas on foreign fuel oil. They were imposed in 1959 during the Eisenhower administration—but only because foreign oil was then cheaper than domestic oil, and many U.S. oil companies wanted that cheap oil kept out. Ironically, the quotas were lifted in 1973—under the Nixon administration—just when they were needed to combat price boosts.

By that time we had used up lots of American oil, which could have been saved, and the rapidly rising world prices were a boon rather than a threat to U.S. oil companies.

Public suspicion of the oil companies and disbelief about oil shortages have not been without foundation. Since the 1920s, oil companies have cried "Shortage!" whenever it suited their purposes—sometimes to help them gain access to foreign oil deposits, sometimes to keep *out* foreign oil, sometimes to *import* oil at high prices, sometimes to freeze out independent companies, sometimes for fear of gluts which would lower prices.

Oil companies have always found patriotic reasons for whatever they recommended. For example, sometimes it was in the national interest to keep our American oil in the ground. On the other hand, sometimes it was in the national interest to keep our American oil wells pumping

"Oh, We're Working Hard On The Oil Situation—We're Holding Down Imports Of Low-Cost Foreign Oil"
3/31/70

"Who Was Navigating, Anyhow?"
6/19/73

"Did You See The Way That Fence Suddenly Hurled Itself At Me?"
11/15/73

"You've Got To Realize, Getting Everything You Want Isn't Everything"
1/22/74

away. The one consistent interest of the oil companies has been to achieve maximum prices and profit.

The multinational oil companies have worked closely with the Organization of Petroleum Exporting Countries (OPEC), and the rising tide of prices has raised the profits of all oil companies.

But despite stacked statistics and cries of "wolf" from oil companies, there *is* a genuine crisis, and it is this: the United States, which used to export oil, was by the late 1970s importing nearly half its supply, thus creating a dependence on foreign oil. Most of the OPEC cartel governments have been non-democratic and have had no regard for the impact on the industrial democracies—except as places to invest their multibillions of petrodollars.

Most of these "Third World" oil-rich countries have also shown little regard for poorer "Third World" nations whose economies were jarred by oil-price inflation too.

In 1973, President Nixon unveiled "Project Independence" and said:

> Let's set as our national goal, in the spirit of Apollo [moon program] and with the determination of the Manhattan [atomic] project, that by the end of the decade we will have developed the potential to meet our own energy needs without depending on any foreign energy sources.

2/17/74

"They Seem To Have Their Own
Rationing System"
1/24/74

"Why Don't You Get Out There And Take Him On?"
5/23/75

"Yup, It's A-Comin' All Right"
6/15/75

"Does Um Kittypoo Want More Yumyums To Tempt His Little Tumtum?"
11/11/75

"Can We Supply Fuel? Leave Everything To Us And We'll Have You Swimming In It"
11/26/75

He also said, "We have an energy crisis but there is no crisis of the American spirit." President Carter, in a 1979 speech on the same subject, told us that there *is* a "crisis of the American spirit."

Whatever the spiritual situation, rhetoric could not be converted to energy and political hot air could not heat homes.

"By the end of the decade"—1980—we were importing far more oil than we had been in 1973.

New oil riches discovered on the North Slope of Alaska did not solve our energy problems either, despite the Nixon administration's desire to give a group of oil companies whatever rights it could to build a trans-Alaska pipeline.

A better alternative would have been an Alaskan-Canadian pipeline, which could have brought oil down to the Great Lakes region where it is most needed.

But the pipeline was built to Valdez, a southern port in Alaska. After an assortment of construction scandals and errors, the pipeline was completed in 1977. The oil then began flowing and was ready to be shipped to California, which at the time didn't need it or want it. Another pipeline—across the United States—then came under consideration to take the oil to—where else?—the Great Lakes region. By this time another U.S. pipeline seemed to be just what we didn't need.

Meanwhile ships ply their courses south from Alaska, laden with

The Flow Begins
7/29/76

11/10/76

"What Do You Mean, 'What's For Tomorrow?' "
11/19/76

"Fireside Chat"
2/3/77

11/30/76

"The Government Said It Wants Sacrifices, Didn't It?"
3/2/77

oil that may or may not spill before reaching ports from which it is then transported to its ultimate destinations.

During the same period, the Nixon administration promoted the building of supertankers, capable of conveying oil—and spilling it—on a larger scale than ever before. However much these ships may have suited the oil companies and the maritime industries, they did not contribute to "energy independence."

The Ford administration went to fight the foe with a continuation of Project Independence. Among other things, his administration called for development of energy-efficient standards for appliances; $2-a-barrel in excise taxes and import fees on petroleum products; revision of Clean Air laws to promote greater use of coal; deregulation of natural gas; removal of price controls on domestic crude oil; and—yes—a windfall profits tax. It even proposed energy tax credits to homeowners who installed insulation. These, in case you're confused, were offered by President Ford, well before the election of Carter.

One feature of the Ford administration proposals was an oil price "floor," which would alleviate domestic producers' fears that OPEC might hurt them by suddenly cutting prices. The administration assumed

4/21/77

"From All The Fuss, We Might As Well Have Proposed Something Tough"
4/24/77

"Down!"
6/12/77

"I Dunno—There's Just No Incentive To Go Out And Try To Fish Up Anything"
8/14/77

"The Reason He's Not Hunting Is Because We Haven't Been Feeding Him Enough"
10/20/77

"I'll Drink To That, Kiddo"
11/8/77

that foreign oil prices, then at $11 a barrel, would level off at about $7 a barrel, or maybe drop to $4 or $5 a barrel. Dreams, dreams, dreams!

During the same Ford administration a Rockefeller report outlined a $100-billion program for fuel alternatives, to be developed largely by big industries themselves. This, like the floor-price proposal, never got off the floor, while prices continued to go through the ceiling.

In looking back over proposals of the 1970s, it is interesting to note how far away 1980 and 1985 seemed to be. Anything ten years away still seems remote.

Solar energy as a practical source of power has often been referred to as something ten to twenty years in the future. Had we begun an "Apollo" solar energy program in the early 1970s, we would now be

"Okay, If You're Sure It Doesn't Go To Uncle Sam"
5/4/77

Leadership
3/5/78

12/8/77

"I Was Doing The Limit When These Trucks Began Rolling Over Me . . ."
12/2/77

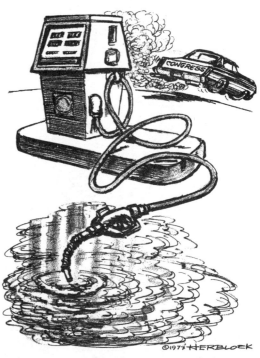

Off And Running
12/18/77

ten years or so closer to a real solar program—even without the advancing technologies that could hasten development. Had a crash program been started in 1977, we would now, in the 1980s, be at least a few years closer to long-term solutions of our energy problems. A crash program was not begun, despite the Jimmy Carter rhetoric.

At his inauguration in January, 1977, Carter's reviewing stand in front of the White House was built with what were described as solar panels in the roof. In the enthusiasm for the new President, and the hope of a new approach to the energy problem, it might have seemed churlish to note that the glass bulges atop the reviewing stand did not actually heat it. They were symbolic—installed to warm the hearts of people who wanted solar energy.

More encouraging was his speech three months later, when he said about coping with the energy problem that, "With the exception of preventing war, this is the greatest challenge that our country will face during our lifetime." And borrowing a phrase originated by Henry James, Carter added, "This difficult effort will be the 'moral equivalent of war.'"

The words were stirring, and many of us responded with enthusiasm. A couple of years later, President Carter would be complaining bitterly

Dear Congress— Please give the Saudi Arabian gentlemen what they want. They are treating me nice, and I promised them you would help out. Enclosed is a photo of me

©1978 HERBLOCK

5/3/78

"If You're Not Going To Move Any Faster, I Might Just Blast Off By Myself"
6/23/78

193

that his reference to "the moral equivalent of war" had been met with ridicule. It had not. The ridicule came later when it turned out that the deeds did not match the bold words.

The U.S. Congress had to share the blame for failure to meet the energy crisis during the 1970s.

Congress conspicuously failed to impose the "wellhead tax" on domestic crude oil that Carter proposed in 1977. The benefits of this were to be tied up with aid to needy consumers through rebates.

Carter's energy plans suffered from two things. First: his penchant for detailed programs which work out well on paper or in a Rube Goldberg cartoon, where pigeon (a) can be counted on to peck at birdseed (b), thereby cutting thread (c), which releases flatiron (d) to fall on walnut (e), and so on.

Such plans, which Carter called "complicated" and "well balanced" might work under governments where a ruler can issue an entire set of decrees. But they don't work so well with a Congress in which various committees and members decide for themselves each item, each tax, each grant of authority.

Second—and even more important—the Carter program was not really bold enough for a "war" on the energy problem.

Consider his 1977 proposal for a gasoline tax of five cents a gallon

"Electric Bill"
8/23/78

Back Burner
12/3/78

for each of five years "that we fail to meet our annual targets"—with the "added incentive" (if you're still following) "that if we miss one year but are back on the track the next, the additional tax would come off."

Compare this with the "tax" imposed by escalating OPEC prices, which raised oil and gasoline costs 100 percent in less than three years—and without rebates or "added incentives."

The U.S. gasoline tax in 1980 was four cents a gallon—the same tax originally set in 1956.

What we were to have was sacrifice without inconvenience—to meet a crisis, sort of.

One of the things President Carter called for and got was a separate Department of Energy, which replaced other agencies dealing with energy.

Thus an even larger bureaucracy was created to make newer and bigger mistakes. The government needed solid information on oil supplies and energy in general. But the Department of Energy still seemed to rely largely on the oil industry for its figures and calculations. It also

"Let Us Know When You Fellows Get Serious"
3/15/78

"We Rub These Sticks Together Till We Strike A Spark . . .
We Keep Rubbing These Sticks Together . . .
We Take These Sticks . . ."
2/1/78

seemed to feel that the oil companies knew best what to do about alternative energy sources.

Who knows more about energy than the energy companies? And who knows more about playing all the angles to benefit the energy companies?

The Department of Energy also poured oil into salt domes as a reserve (something previously recommended by President Ford). However, the DOE didn't initially install the necessary pumps to get the oil *out*.

President Ford had proposed a petroleum reserve of 500 million barrels by 1982. Carter talked of a goal of one billion barrels. But by March, 1980, we had managed to store less than 91 million barrels—the equivalent of less than two weeks' supply of oil imports. One factor was Saudi Arabia's displeasure with selling us oil that we might salt away for the future.

The government kept telling us we were in an emergency, but it didn't build up an emergency reserve. So much for "the greatest challenge that our country will face during our lifetime."

As people waited in gas lines in 1979, the Department of Energy gave out statements that were like "uppers and downers" in predicting both tighter gasoline supplies and more plentiful supplies. These varying statements were apparently designed to impress Americans with the seriousness of the situation and then to reassure them that they needn't get excited. These forecasts sounded as if they were determined by spinning a bottle.

While all this was going on, columns by Mike Causey of *The Wash-*

**"We Already Have Alternate
Energy Sources"**
1/30/79

**"You Sure You Wouldn't Care To Sit
Down Over Here?"**
2/18/79

"Hit Me Again"
3/28/79

"So Far, So Good"
5/3/79

"Schlesinger Here—What Can I Do For You Today?"
5/10/79

"And You'll Be Sure To Let Us Know When You Think We Should Develop Alternate Energy Sources"
6/13/79

ington Post disclosed that the U.S. government itself was a great waster of gas. As one example, it used vans to shuttle one or two employees a couple of blocks and deadhead back. A principal offender was the Department of Energy.

Meanwhile, on another energy front, Carter had vacillated on the issue of deregulating natural gas, but eventually went along with Congress on it. He also began the deregulation of oil prices, to be accompanied by a windfall profits tax on oil companies.

When the Carter administration decided to get into big numbers, it proposed a program reminiscent of the Ford–Rockefeller proposal—$80 billion (in one speech Carter spoke of $140 billion) to come out of windfall taxes for a "synfuels" program. The "synfuels" program is essentially a plan to press more oil and gas out of coal, shale, and rocks.

This program—which Congress knocked down to $20 billion to start —did not include large-scale development of solar energy or many promising alternate methods of getting at new gas and oil. Gasohol did not get a big play until the Russian invasion of Afghanistan in 1979. The administration protested by curtailing wheat shipments to Russia. And partly to mollify concerned farmers, it suddenly developed a greater interest in a large gasohol program.

"What'll It Be—Odd Or Even?"
6/22/79

Preacher's Pulpit
3/15/79

Now Playing
6/26/79

7/25/79

8/3/79

**"And We Hereby Initiate Our New
Alternate Energy Sources Program"**
6/21/79

The multibillion-dollar energy program also neglected development of sources in poorer areas of the world where new energy riches, developed with our aid, could be shared.

This program also overlooked the potential of energy from solid waste. What we had was fuel waste.

The immediate need, in this continuing crisis, was fuel conservation. Through three administrations the U.S. government had, all printed up in case of emergency, gasoline rationing coupons. And through three administrations there was a horror of using them. In 1979, Congress even adopted its own special provisions for restraining or preventing gas rationing if somebody in the White House should go wild and adopt such an idea.

There is no way of meeting the energy crisis that entails no sacrifices

"I Keep Having This Feeling That I've Met You Before"
10/22/78

"It's Much Faster"
10/30/79

"The Main Thing Is To Avoid Giving It To Our Own Government"
5/15/80

and that is completely equitable. Rationing by price is not absolutely fair—especially to people who don't have an interest in oil companies. Stiff gasoline taxes wouldn't be entirely fair, even if the government tried to return the money to needier consumers. But import quotas and duties, gas taxes and rationing—any or all of these—are better than paying out ever-increasing amounts to oil-exporting countries and to oil companies.

Carter, in the spring of 1980, finally announced application of an oil import fee, which would have raised gasoline prices about ten cents a gallon. Gerald Ford had applied an import fee in 1975, although it was later lifted because of congressional disapproval. Carter's import fee-gas tax ran into opposition in Congress and in the courts.

Saudi Arabia has been regarded as one of the more moderate and friendly oil exporters. In the summer of 1979, President Carter asked the government of that country to please increase its available oil to us for a time. The Saudi foreign minister obliged, and in a communication shortly before the Fourth of July, he told a grateful Carter that this was his "Independence Day present."

This was not independence; it was not the moral equivalent of war; it was a great nation on its knees. ∎

"It Gets Into Everything"
7/15/79

THE RULERS OF IRAN

OVER THE YEARS the rulers of Iran have searched for wide influence and power. The Shah Mohammad Reza Pahlavi sought it through vastly increased oil income, through rapid modernization, and through huge purchases of the most modern and sophisticated military planes and weaponry. The Shah envisioned Iran as a mighty Persia and himself as a great world leader. He was, for all practical purposes, a military ally of the United States, and our policy toward him was simple. We gave him—or sold him—anything he wanted. It made no difference that he was one who led the way in quadrupling the price of OPEC oil to us. In fact, the higher oil prices enabled the Shah to buy the sophisticated arms our government was eager to sell him. The Shah, on the other

"Explain Slowly—What Does He Need All
Those Weapons For, And Why Does He
Need Nuclear Reactors?"
3/20/75

"You Don't Realize How Warm I Get
Doing All This Cooking"
5/20/75

"We Were Ready For Anything Except
Iranians With Rocks And Bricks"
1/3/79

"The Dictatorship Is Gone! Bring On
The Dictatorship!"
1/19/79

hand, kept the oil taps open during the 1973 embargo. We considered
Iran, under the Shah, our great bastion in the Persian Gulf region.

The dictatorship that replaced the Shah also saw itself as a power in
the world. It also counted on riding "a wave of oil," but its ambitions
were to lead a wave of Moslem resurgence in the world, spreading its
religious and revolutionary influence abroad.

The revolution in Iran that gathered momentum in December, 1978,
was directed against the Shah, who had succeeded his father's rule in
1941. In 1951, Mohammed Mossadegh became prime minister of Iran.
In 1953 he engaged in a power struggle with the Shah, whom he tried to
arrest. The Shah fled the country but returned within a week, when he
was restored to power with the help of the CIA.

The revolutionaries, who took over in February, 1979, accused the
Shah of massive corruption and of responsibility for tortures and murders
by his secret police, the SAVAK. Rebelling Iranians, directed by the
Ayatollah Ruhollah Khomeini, went on strike, demonstrated, shut down
oil wells, and brought the country to a halt. The Shah made concessions
and appointed a prime minister who he hoped would unify the country,
but to no avail. In January, 1979, the Shah left Iran. The Ayatollah
returned from exile to the acclaim of frenzied mobs.

It is worth a note in passing that whatever the crimes committed under
the Shah, his arch-enemy Khomeini had not been executed or hunted

Spiritual Leader
4/8/79

**"This Is Nothing Like The Shah's Rule—
We Don't Wear Fancy Hats And Epaulets"**
4/19/79

Bath
5/11/79

Trial
11/22/79

down, but allowed to live in exile. Khomeini and his followers, who accused the Shah of torture, murder, and other crimes, wanted the death of the Shah and all members of the Shah's family. A nephew of the Shah was, in fact, assassinated in Paris in December, 1979.

Khomeini approved and encouraged executions, with trials that consisted only of judges, accusers, and defendants. We do not know how many of the executed were indeed members of the SAVAK, who had engaged in torture and murder. Dozens of women were executed for prostitution or adultery. Death sentences were also imposed for homosexuality or other offenses against the mores of the revolutionists. In the trials, it was explained that the judges' identities were kept secret for their (the judges) protection.

This contempt for western standards of justice was only part of Khomeini's revolution against western ways, which included western culture, western dress for women, western ideas of freedom, and even the playing of music.

Khomeini—in his holy-war style—spoke literally of Satan, whom he claimed was the United States or its leader.

There was, in all this, a method to his madness. Iran was not only in trouble economically but was also facing opposition from dissidents and groups seeking autonomy within the country. He was not the first national leader to find it advantageous to focus the nation's attention on an outside "enemy."

Embassy Row
11/25/79

11/29/79

207

Hostage
11/15/79

A plebiscite was held, by non-secret ballot, making Iran an Islamic state and making Khomeini "spiritual ruler for life"—with power above any elected officials.

Under Islamic law, as explained by the government in Iran, Iran was ruled by the word of God, with Khomeini the interpreter of God's word.

On November 4, 1979, an Iranian mob invaded American territory— our embassy in Tehran—seized the embassy and took fifty prisoners, thenceforth referred to as "hostages." Three other Americans were held hostage at the Foreign Ministry.

The seizure of the American embassy was supposedly triggered by the admission of the Shah to the United States for medical treatment.

The action of the terrorists, generally referred to in Iran as "students," was approved and apparently encouraged by Khomeini. Together they demanded that the Shah be returned to them for trial and execution. This was the asking price for release of the Americans.

Our government refused to surrender the Shah. But after the Shah left the U.S. hospital, he went to Panama. And when he needed another operation, it was President Anwar Sadat who welcomed him to Egypt for medical services and a place to live. President Carter, who had extravagant praise for the Shah when he ruled Iran, did not provide the exiled Shah with refuge or even additional medical service in the United States.

So the Carter administration had not surrendered the Shah—but it

"Pay No Attention To The Empty Thrones, Imam"
12/4/79

"I Know You're All Tired, But Let's Shake Those Fists Again, And Don't Burn Today's Uncle Sam Effigy Till The Cameras Roll—Okay—Action—"
12/12/79

"Is There Anyone We've Forgotten?"
1/6/80

Iran Calendar
2/21/80

"And Now The Latest From Terroran"
12/27/79

"It's Another Story Referring To The Terrorists Over There As 'Students' "
12/23/79

did not want to give offense to the Shah's successor, who thirsted for the Shah's blood.

At the beginning of this crisis, President Carter froze Iranian assets in the United States. He also announced that imports of oil from Iran were being stopped. Carter threatened economic sanctions by the United States and its allies, but later delayed them.

In one of his first reactions to the seizure, Carter said that the United States would not respond with force—but he later suggested that, if all else failed, we might have to resort to non-peaceful methods.

Under President Carter, the United States itself became hostage to the Iranian situation.

The American government and people remained preoccupied with the holding of the hostages from the day they were seized. Night after night on TV, Americans saw Iranian mobs, in organized demonstrations, chanting "Death to the U.S.!" "Death to Carter!" Week after week there were televised interviews with families of the hostages. And some of the hostages appeared in film clips taken and edited by their captors and provided to American networks.

In the Iranian government, ministers came and went, and nothing was certain except the power of Khomeini and the "students" holding the American embassy.

In the United States, there were candlelight vigils, bells were rung, and prayers were conducted for the hostages. In December, 1979, the President lit only a part of the national Christmas tree in Washington, to show that he cared for the hostages—even if such acts did nothing for the hostages or our position in the world. In an official reaction, the government ordered the registration of Iranian students in the United States and said that any found to be here illegally would be deported. This procedure, questioned by civil libertarians, was apparently designed to relieve the tensions of Americans goaded by some Iranian students here who were pro-Khomeini.

While everyone was concerned for the hostages' lives, not everyone considered how the nation should respond to terrorism and attacks by foreign rulers. It seemed to be taken for granted that if we displeased the leaders in Iran by a show of force, the hostages would be executed. Threats from practically any source were taken at face value. It was also generally assumed that if the hostages were eventually released, even after months of captivity, they would be all right, so long as they had not been "mistreated."

The captivity itself was mistreatment. The invasion of the U.S. embassy was an act of war, and we could have regarded it as such to any extent that we chose.

Other consulates and embassies were attacked elsewhere. In the capital of Pakistan, the American embassy was burned to the ground. Two

American servicemen lost their lives. And some fifty people in that embassy managed to avoid incineration only because they were lucky enough to find a hatch through which they managed to escape.

The number of Americans who nearly burned to death in that embassy was about the same as the number of hostages in Tehran.

As the weeks after weeks after weeks went by with the captives still being held, the Carter administration backed down time after time on things it had said it would not stand for. Carter said there would be no negotiations about anything until the hostages were released. After abandoning this position, he retreated from other "firm" positions regarding the hostages.

But for a long time, the President's policy had wide popular support.

After months of frustration, Americans received some news to cheer about.

The Canadian embassy in Tehran had secretly sheltered some American diplomats. When the Canadians shut their embassy down, they provided the Americans with Canadian credentials and brought them safely past Iranian officials.

The Canadian embassy staff and the six rescued Americans returned home to the acclaim and thanks of all Americans. The foreign minister of Iran protested that the whole procedure violated International Law.

"And Now, Especially For Sadegh
Ghotbzadeh, Of Tehran, Iran—
The Maple Leaf Rag"
2/1/80

Item: Administration Plans For Increased
Use Of Coal In Northern U.S. May Cause
"Acid Rain" Across Border
2/12/80

In Iran, Abol Hassan Bani-Sadr was elected president. He and the foreign minister called for removal of the Americans from the U.S. embassy, and the terrorist "students" had agreed. But nothing ever remained agreed upon for long. Despite previous understandings, a UN commission came and went without seeing the hostages.

After more than five months, Iranian officials allowed two Red Cross representatives to see the American prisoners, but not to interview them privately in accordance with customary Red Cross practice.

As one newspaper pointed out, the Shah in 1977–78 was freer in giving Red Cross representatives access to his prisoners under the usual Red Cross conditions.

Five months after the seizure of our embassy, the United States finally broke diplomatic relations with Iran.

Two and a half weeks later—on April 25, 1980—President Carter told the nation that there had been an attempted American rescue mission to Iran, which had taken place the night before and failed. An American

"More Leeches, More Bleeding, Stronger Potions!"
11/13/79

force, in helicopters and planes, had been dispatched to the Iranian desert. But three helicopters malfunctioned. One helicopter collided with one of our planes, and both burst into flames, resulting in the death of eight American servicemen. The mission was aborted, all the helicopters and the burned plane were abandoned, and the remaining Americans were evacuated in planes.

A diplomatic casualty of this venture was Secretary of State Cyrus Vance, who opposed the mission. He was later replaced by Senator Edmund Muskie.

Carter, who did not rule out further action of some kind, euphemistically called the fiasco in Iran an "incomplete success." It was an ill-planned and ill-timed venture—a complete failure.

Time had not run in favor of an erratic policy that was consistent only in keeping the hostage situation in the limelight. After the USSR's December, 1979, move into Afghanistan brought the Soviets to the Iranian border, our government's fear of Russian support of Iran or of

"Sit!"
4/13/80

"The Japanese Sent Us This Electronic Computer"
4/23/80

214

its intervention there made matters more difficult for us. Bold moves taken early might have been easier.

Meanwhile Khomeini had announced that the hostage situation would await the election of a parliament. And the parliament would decide . . .

Khomeini and his "revolutionary guard" and his "student" terrorists were in no hurry. The holding of the hostages was their day, their week, their month-after-month in the sun. For more than half a year, they were the focus of world attention. The hostages were like money in the bank.

Khomeini seemed to have more to fear from disorders and new revolutionary struggles at home than from American force or international actions.

Meanwhile, what other terrorists in what other places might be making future plans to get so much attention, with so much toleration of their actions for so long without effective counter measures? ∎

Panel
2/26/80

"Sixth Month"
4/27/80

OF SPECIAL INTEREST
FOR SOME

THERE ARE FEW aphorisms more often quoted than Samuel Johnson's observation on mental concentration—so look out, here it comes again. "Nothing," he said, "so concentrates a man's mind as the knowledge that he is to be hanged in the morning."

I wouldn't have brought it up except for the special-interests groups that concentrate on putting into a politician's mind the knowledge that at the next election his career can be dead.

One of the longest-running of the single-interest groups is the gun lobby. It goes under the sporting name of the National Rifle Association but devotes itself largely to trying to prevent any registration or control over handguns. The handgun is the favored weapon of criminals who seldom give their victims a sporting chance.

But the NRA does not limit itself to preventing identification of guns used by criminals. It has also fought to prevent identification of explosives, which can now be "marked" with tracers. In a bombing murder, for example, detectives have been able to trace the dynamite to the buyer. The National Rifle Association does not wish to spoil the sport of people whose carrying and use of explosives could be identified.

The gun lobby has even been able to get subsidies from the U.S. government. The Defense Department has for years given free guns and millions of rounds of ammunition to civilians to practice shooting. In order to participate in these "defense" programs, the civilians had to be members of the NRA. It thus gained more members and more membership funds. This direct support of the gun lobby has cost the Defense Department over half a million dollars a year.

By a coincidence, the National Rifle Association spent some half a million dollars in congressional elections in 1978. Thus, the executive branch of the U.S. government in effect contributed to the efforts of a lobby to shoot down members of the legislative branch.

But politicians who backed down on gun control legislation may have been keeling over at the shooting of mere blanks. Public opinion polls continue to show an overwhelming support for handgun controls—even by a majority of *owners* of handguns. The Pentagon has tired of giving money to the NRA gun lobby. And when the NRA takes aim at congressmen who are on their election hit lists, it has not been scoring so well in recent years.

The NRA, which had opposed the elections of Congressman Abner Mikva of Illinois, arrayed its full artillery against him in 1979 when he was nominated for a federal judgeship. The gun lobby managed to muster a number of votes against him. But he was approved by the Judiciary Committee and confirmed by the U.S. Senate. In this showdown at the U.S. corral, the NRA did not make out OK.

A group that has increased rapidly in strength is the anti-abortion lobby. It is made up mostly of sincere people who are sure that they are carrying out God's will. They oppose abortion even when sanctioned by laws upheld by the United States Supreme Court.

Some anti-abortionists have not only engaged in public demonstrations but have invaded legal abortion clinics, screamed at women who appeared at the clinics, and in some cases committed acts of violence. They thus added to the trauma of women attending such clinics.

The effects on many members of Congress have also been traumatic.

"Fair Enough—Let's Give Them A Cut Out Of What
We Take Tonight"
5/25/75

**"What—Put Numbers On Guns,
As If They Could Be Used In Crimes
Like Automobiles?"**
5/25/78

"Nobody Here But Just Us Sportsmen"
3/3/76

Creation Of Life
2/20/75

**"It's Very Simple—If You Could Afford
Children, You Could Have Abortions"**
6/21/77

The U.S. House of Representatives has regularly voted to deny public funds for abortions even in cases of rape or incest. In 1979, the House also tried to prevent the District of Columbia from using any of its *own* locally raised tax funds for such purposes.

Powerful groups beget opposition groups. The "Right-to-Life" people find themselves opposed by those who believe women should have "Freedom-of-Choice." Congressmen who feel it is safest to string along with the anti-abortion lobby may find they guessed wrong about the strength of those who oppose it.

Veterans among the lobbies are most of the veterans' organizations themselves. Many "professional veterans" want to have it both ways— they served their country with no thought but that of patriotism, *BUT* they want all the payment they can keep wringing out of the country. There is certainly a national obligation to aid those disabled in the line of duty, but benefits and pensions for veterans who have incurred disabilities in no way connected with service are simply handouts.

There are more than 500 corporations and over 1,500 trade and professional associations in Washington, outnumbering members of Congress by about four to one.

"You Ain't Gonna Close Your Pocketbooks
To Us Veterans, Are You?"
8/16/78

6/21/78

"Another Good Crop This Year"
1/12/78

**"Please—No Interference With The Sacred
Patient-Dollar Relationship"**
6/27/79

"Tsk Tsk—Accidents Will Happen"
4/2/76

**"—And If Elected, I Promise Not Only To
Outlaw School Busing, But To Outlaw
The Schools Too"**
5/9/72

Among professional groups one of the most successful has been the American Trial Lawyers Association. More than once it has prevented passage of a no-fault insurance bill. The members of this lobby are not all ambulance chasers. They are dollar chasers. And they don't want anything to interfere with their making the maximum.

The American Medical Association and hospital association lobbies had an interest in opposing Carter administration proposals for limiting hospital costs. When it comes to legislation on medical matters, these groups want Congress to deliver just what the doctors order.

The National Education Association has often lobbied for good causes. But in 1979 President Carter and a majority of Congress obliged this lobby by adding to the federal bureaucracy a Department of Education —despite the fact that public education is not essentially a federal function, much less one that requires a separate cabinet-level department.

Congressmen are generally aware of agricultural or agribusiness interests within their states. The sugar lobby is influential even though Congress does not always sweeten the pot exactly to the taste of that lobby.

The tobacco lobby has a natural constituency in tobacco-growing states, but it also has the funds to reach beyond those areas. It spends large amounts to defeat measures in any state that would call for any indoor non-smoking areas. The White House has been mindful that the tobacco industry has votes in Congress and has money to spend—and that it also produces revenue at home and helps with the trade balance through sales abroad. President Carter made clear that tobacco growers were among his constituents and showed no desire either to fight the industry or to switch the farmers to other crops.

Industrial lobbies fight all forms of pollution control. And the energy crisis has provided them with an excuse for trying to scuttle clean air and water standards. Rigor mortis saves energy.

Another form of environmental pollution is represented by the can-and-bottle lobbies, which firmly resist any legislation to discourage the use of throwaway containers. Going back to the old American custom of using returnable bottles is something they find practically un-American.

Despite the fact that some states have curbed throwaways with considerable success and with general public approval, the throwaway lobbies keep insisting that their costly, energy-wasting, and eyesore disposables are some kind of national treasure.

Through the magic mirrors of television many of these lobbies show us how beneficial and public-spirited they are.

The container lobby, for example, runs commercials showing how kids running around the littered landscape can pick up sacks full of used containers, and how these containers, when eventually returned, cleaned

"Still Want To Help All Those Common People?"
5/2/80

and crunched up, can be used to manufacture *new* throwaway containers —*saving ENERGY*!

What they don't explain is how much more energy might be saved if the containers were returned directly—and, in the case of bottles, used over again—all without using still more energy to retrieve all those cans and bottles in all their versatile disposability.

The influence of the oil lobby is all-pervasive. The oil companies not only exercise generous influence in Congress, they spend generously on ads, which are particularly effective on TV. They show how clean and ship-shape their vessels are, how their offshore and onshore work actually enhances the environment and provides happier places for fish to swim and birds to fly—and all this to provide us with *more energy*. These clean ads are paid for out of billions of dollars of clean profit.

An assortment of interests make up a powerful maritime lobby. Steel companies, shipbuilders, shipyard districts, and shipping unions are among those who give the taxpayer an added going-over on the water-front. Besides having strong representation in Congress, the maritime industry is also heavily represented in the Department of Commerce.

This lobby also goes in for TV ads. These show ships flying American flags, which make their commercials very patriotic and colorful.

"Talk About Wastrels!"
9/6/77

The Final Throwaway
6/24/75

"I Hope You People Won't Be Demagogic"
7/31/77

Name Of The Game
8/12/79

Greased Pigs
6/30/77

**"Let's Hear It For The Fairest One
Of All"**
12/12/73

When President Carter came into office, he proposed a consumer agency, at a modest cost to the taxpayer. To hear the screams from all the special interests that influence Congress and the executive department, you'd think that such an agency would sweep away everything that had built up America. The proposal met stiff resistance in Congress, and the Carter administration fell back to Plan B, which was to mumble approval and let the proposed agency fall by the wayside.

But consumers found a champion in the Federal Trade Commission, a formerly comatose regulatory agency that had finally started to show a vigorous interest in protecting the public. This resulted in demands from several special interests—and the congressmen who spoke the lines for them—that the FTC be sharply curbed.

Among those many interests fighting against FTC proposals were

"Your Energy Bill Is In The Pipeline"
10/26/77

225

"Help! I'm In Danger Of Being Run Down!"
2/3/78

"I'm Against Things Being Regulated"
12/26/79

"We Find This Regulatory Agency Guilty Of Acting Like A Regulatory Agency"
11/30/79

"You Don't Know What It Is To Find You've Stretched Yourself Too Far In Buying An Extra 500 Acres—And Another Hundred Grand Of New Equipment . . ."
2/7/79

used-car dealers, who saw no need to inform purchasers of any defects in what they were selling. The multi-billion-dollar insurance companies saw no reason why people should be interested in studies showing how much interest they were actually getting on their insurance policy savings. Then there was the funeral business, which did not want to be regulated to the point of having to give the bereaved a price list or itemizations of charges—or an honest accounting of whether embalming, for example, is required (or NOT required) by law.

Such requirements may sound reasonable to consumers, but they outrage the interests that would be obliged to level with customers. These groups would like the FTC's regulations to have the nicest, most elaborate, and expensive funeral anywhere, with the remains placed in a special vault—not just for months—or for years—but for eternity.

Public-interest groups as well as private-interest groups have a stake in regulations. Where regulations don't suit, the groups want backing in legislation. We're all familiar with the cry, "There ought to be a law!"

"They're Claiming It Would Make Us Subject To Combat Duty"
11/18/77

It takes laws even to repeal laws. But when laws aren't passed or don't do the job, there is a call for something else: "There ought to be an amendment!"

For years, some constitutional amendments have tried to make their way through the required number of states, and even more have tried to make their way through Congress.

The Equal Rights Amendment fell short of the required number of states before the original seven years designated for its passage, and Congress gave it an extension of time.

An amendment for the popular election of president and vice-president —without the old electoral college crowd—has been talked about after almost every presidential election. Such an amendment finally came to the floor of the Senate in 1979. It was defeated largely by a coalition of those who thought it would diminish the importance of small states in elections and those who thought it would diminish the importance of minority votes.

I think the president should be elected by direct vote of the people, with each person's vote counting for exactly as much as any other person's. That doesn't diminish anyone's rights.

"Now To Go Through The Suggestion Box"
11/2/76

"Made It—And Hope You'll Try Your Luck With Us Again On Your Next Trip"
11/9/76

Among other proposed amendments are some providing for prayer in the public schools—meaning designated prayer or time designated for prayer. I don't know what's wrong with prayer at home, prayer at church, or silent prayer anywhere, without special designated school time to separate the true believers from the non-participants. But a lot of people think the public school is the place to learn prayer and to see who's praying and who isn't.

There are also proposed anti-abortion amendments, which would embed the anti-abortion idea into the basic fabric of government.

Then there are various proposals for a balance-the-budget amendment. Governor Jerry Brown of California thought that one was worth a constitutional convention. I've never understood how a budget-balancing amendment would work—much less how a constitutional convention would operate. Oddly enough there has been no move for an amendment to repeal the Sixteenth Amendment. That one, which was controversial in its day, gave the federal government the power to levy an income tax.

This brings us to a proposed amendment—passed by Congress and making the rounds of the states—in which *I* have a special interest. But

1/18/79

"It's Not A Bird, Not A Plane—
It's Stuperman!"
1/11/79

it is the same interest that motivated the founders who protested against taxation without representation. That is the amendment to provide voting representation in Congress for the residents of the District of Columbia. This is where I live—and the non-representation hits me where I live too.

We pay the federal income tax and a local income tax higher than almost any state in the union. This is in addition to all other federal and local taxes. There are at least four states with smaller populations than the District of Columbia. District residents are drafted when there are drafts, and they fight and die in wars when there are wars. But they have no voting representation in the Congress that passes the tax bills or the draft laws or anything else.

Opposition to the D.C. amendment comes mostly from those who don't want to give the vote to an area that is predominantly black, and from those who don't want to "dilute" their influences in the House and Senate by giving representation to other Americans.

That amendment is my special interest. Those who believe in basic citizenship rights for all Americans should have a special interest in it too. ■

"Ah, Independence Day—The Glorious Fourth! Do See
That The Natives Get A Nice Fireworks Display"
6/30/78

"He's Quite Independent—Of Political Leadership, That Is"
8/8/78

231

THE WORLD AT LARGE

IN WORLD AFFAIRS the United States has gone through eras of isolation, cooperation, and confrontation. Lately, we have been in the Era of Frustration.

We are no longer the post-WW-II Superman flying around the world defending right and helping those in need. The days when we helped rebuild the countries of friends and former foes are today old newsreel clips.

We now lag behind some of those countries in the rate of growth of productivity. We see in the UN dozens of new Third World countries that have not grown up to be the free democratic cooperative nations we hoped for. Many of them act as if they'd prefer that we walk on the

Hunger
11/17/74

"Remember When There Used To Be
Quaint Countries And Faraway Places?"
2/15/79

"Ingrates! You Let Them Vote And The Next Thing, They Want Their Ballots Counted"
4/12/78

"Fidel Certainly Makes Sure We Don't Have An Unemployment Problem"
2/9/78

"Right, Strom—What We've Got To Do Is Keep The Canal And Give The Rest Away"
9/9/77

"Synchronize Watches—If The Concorde Is Not Given Landing Rights, France Is At War With New York"
3/8/77

2/25/77

Dark Torch
9/6/72

Pusher
8/3/76

"Stick With Me—I've Got A System"
8/7/75

other side of the street, and they are often on the other side from us in UN votes.

Even the Philippines, which grew up under our tutelage, gained freedom only to go under a military dictatorship. Vietnam, for all our firepower, didn't work out. And we suffer an oil squeeze from nouveau-riche countries that treat us in the manner of wealthy landlords who might shut off the gas of a delinquent tenant.

For the past few years, we've been going through a lot of self-analysis.

By now I think we'd better get off the couch and stop feeling so guilty, guilty, guilty about having gone into Vietnam that we will never, never, never raise a hand against anyone, under any circumstances. The United States is not, as they say, the policeman of the world. But we shouldn't pull down the shades and plug our ears when muggings are going on either.

We can also dispense with the dreamy notion that if we get back to giving some 007 agency unlimited secret power, it will solve our problems abroad. It never did before, and it won't now. Politicians who tell us that we must deal with the world as it is and not as we'd like it to be, can give up their own cloak-and-dagger fantasies.

We do have to deal with the world as it is. And we can also work to make it what we want it to be.

"The **Old** CIA Would Have Kept The Russians Out Of Afghanistan—The Same As It Kept Them Out Of Czechoslovakia, Hungary, Cuba . . ."
2/3/80

"Hey, Brother—Watch Us Make Those Big Industrial Democracies Jump"
12/20/79

Editing Job
7/27/75

"Who's The Fairest One Of All?"
6/27/75

Johnny Mushroomseed
7/20/76

Plane Ramp
1/13/77

To those who try to present every international crisis as a choice between nuclear war and national paralysis, the correct answer is "neither of the above."

There is nothing too bellicose or overbearing about standing for freedom in the world—and we can begin by making sure we set the best possible example at home.

What we need is a map of our place in the world that says YOU ARE HERE. Other countries could use one too.

India, for example, has gone from democracy to Indiracracy, to democracy, back to Indira and whatever next.

With more U.S. help than we may have realized, India developed what it called a "peaceful" nuclear device. Pakistan has worked toward an "Islamic bomb." There will be others. This proliferation of nuclear weapons is one of two shadows that has been walking the world.

The other lengthening shadow is the spread of terror, indiscriminate bombings, and shootings by organizations and gangs—Red Brigades in Italy, Palestinian terrorist groups, Germany's Baader-Meinhof gang, Japanese Red Army terrorists, Irish Republican Army killers, Puerto Rican FALN members. Besides the random killings of civilians, there have been abductions and murders of government officials, seizings of embassies, and taking of hostages.

The possibility of a combination of such terrorists with any of an

"We Should Be Getting Our International Diplomatic Invitations Any Day Now"
8/11/77

"My Country, Too, Disapproves Of Terrorist Activities—However, We See No Need To Act Hastily . . ."
11/1/77

**"We Too Have Troublemakers Who Don't
Appreciate Authority"**
10/19/71

"Some Of Those Greek Ruins Are Moving"
10/25/74

"We'll Just Sit Tight"
2/10/77

Apartheid
10/21/77

increasing number of atomic bombs is one of the most chilling prospects in the world.

However, the State of the World has not been all bleak. And despite "wars and rumors of wars," there have been many bright spots.

Greece, ruled by a military clique that our government found congenial, threw out its dictators and returned to freedom. The Greek people did it on their own.

Spain emerged from the Franco dictatorship, with which we had long cooperated, to move on toward democracy—and not the communism that had so long been feared.

Portugal, formerly another tight dictatorship, did the same.

Rhodesian peace had been practically written off as a lost cause. But under the direction of British Foreign Minister Lord Carrington, Rhodesia held an election that did not turn out to be the farce many pundits had feared. It became Zimbabwe.

Relations with China were "normalized." Unfortunately, there was also a Chinese "normalization" of Peking's "freedom wall," where once they had let a thousand posters bloom. An official frost nipped the blooming of unauthorized sentiments.

We can also take some satisfaction in noting that some of the sup-

"Let's Start Over—Hua's On First?"
11/26/78

"What's Showing Today?"
12/10/78

"Waiter—Another Cuba Libre"
9/6/79

posed Russian gains in Africa and elsewhere have come unstuck. And Cuba is a Russian dependent that requires costly support.

One of the ironies of recent world events is that Castro's Cuba hosted a meeting of "nonaligned nations" in 1979. (The following year, masses of Cubans fled their country in an effort to be non-aligned with Castro's Cuba.) These "nonaligned" or Third World countries include a variety of rich and poor, some democratic but mostly non-democratic.

Under the Carter administration we had, at first, what amounted to three secretaries of state—one for each world.

We had Secretary Cyrus Vance, National Security Adviser Zbigniew Brzezinski, and UN Ambassador Andrew Young. Young seemed to be Secretary-for-Third-World-Countries. He succeeded in reaching a better rapport with many of these countries and in dispelling notions that the USA was a kind of ITT affiliate. However, he was sometimes given to pleasing these countries by tossing off statements which created other misconceptions about the United States and its policies. He said, "There are hundreds, perhaps thousands of political prisoners [in jails] in the United States." He declared that "the Cuban [troops] bring a certain stability and order to Angola." He predicted the Ayatollah Khomeini would be seen as "some kind of saint." He also said, "I do not see any difference in the so-called due process in Florida [where murderer John

"It Was Entirely Accidental, Sort-of"
8/15/79

8/21/79

"Now The Kindling"
10/28/79

**"It's A Pleasure To Recognize
A Fellow Idealist"**
1/12/75

**"As We Said At Helsinki, We Retain
Control Over Internal Matters"**
11/23/75

Leader Of The Free World
6/12/79

Spcnkclink had recently been tried, found guilty, and executed] and the so-called due process of the Ayatollah Khomeini."

Such remarks required corrections by the United States government. Ambassador Young's resignation was finally accepted, because he was not truthful to his superiors in the State Department in telling them about negotiations he had been conducting.

This left Brzezinski and Vance, along with President Carter, to deal with the various worlds by themselves.

7/19/78

"And Now—Over Here Please—Our
Special Chinese Surprise!"
12/17/78

"He's Got A Real Firm Handshake"
1/31/79

"Of Course We Believe In Détente—
What Other Government Is Responsible
For So Much Detention?"
9/3/78

"I Wouldn' Let You Down, Li'l Pal—
You Wouldn' Let Me Down, Wouldja?"
4/17/79

They reacted to the Russian invasion of Afghanistan in 1979—which Carter called the greatest threat to peace since World War II—by curbing grain shipments to Russia and by stopping export of certain technological equipment. They also proposed the boycotting of the Moscow Olympics of 1980, and someone hastened to proclaim a "Carter Doctrine"—resistance of further Russian expansion in the Persian Gulf area. The latter sounded much like what a U.S. senator had dubbed the "Eisenhower Doctrine" of 1957—resisting the spread of communism in this same general area. In an emergency, every presidential observer must ask, "Is there a doctrine in the house?"

As part of this doctrine, the Carter administration announced that it would give $400 million in military aid to Pakistan, on the Afghanistan border. Dictator Mohammed Zia ul-Haq spurned this first offer as "peanuts" and later rejected *any* American military aid.

Like so many Carter policy initiatives, this one was proposed without consulting the countries affected. It was simply announced. In this case it was announced despite our own policy of showing disapproval of Zia's development of a nuclear bomb.

Failures to consult allies have often been matched by failures to consult Congress. And policies have been abandoned as unpredictably as they were first proclaimed.

Such sudden announcements and sudden changes of policy create for us an international incredibility gap.

"Thank Goodness Everything Has
Cleared Up"
6/13/78

"That's Strange—It Seems To Be Empty"
3/9/78

245

1/3/80

"We Had To Go Into Afghanistan To
Protect Our Southern Border. Now, To
Protect Afghanistan's Borders—"
1/15/80

"Here's A Month-Old Paper That Says
The Peace-Loving Russians Are Moving
Some Of Their Tanks Out Of
East Germany"
1/8/80

"We Might Not Be Able To Control Our
Own People, But We Can Handle Guys
Like This"
2/6/80

The Carter administration moved in strange ways its wonder of confusion to perform.

When it announced, in 1979, the discovery of Russian combat troops in Cuba, our government publicly proclaimed this situation "unacceptable"—strong diplomatic language implying strong action. A couple of weeks later, our government decided that whatever it had found in Cuba was acceptable after all.

After the seizure of our embassy in Iran, President Carter went back and forth on how our government would act—or not act—and on what it wanted our allies to do.

Flip-flops on what our government will tolerate led other countries to assume that if they don't like a Washington policy, it will, like the Washington weather, change after a while.

In the negotiations on our relations with China, there was no need for the Chinese even to wait for a change. Our negotiators, it turned out, did not request a guarantee that China would not use force against Taiwan. They were so afraid the idea would be rejected that they didn't even ask.

One of the worst examples of the Carter administration's weakness in foreign dealings involved a shocking incident in Washington itself.

General Augusto Pinochet's dictatorship in Chile made it one of

"Remember The Good Old Days When We Only Worried About Russia Getting One?"
6/25/74

Foreign Exchange
2/15/78

"As Comrade Brezhnev Says—They're A Tiny Few With No Following, So We Have To Keep Them From Overthrowing The Government"
3/24/77

"And, Oh Yes, A Note From Secretary Vance Deploring Our Position On Iran"
12/9/79

Second Time Around
1/9/80

Ballot Boxed
1/8/78

the worst violators of human rights in Latin America. With Pinochet's secret police, DINA, operating effectively, many Chileans were suddenly missing or their bodies found in abandoned mine shafts.

Orlando Letelier, former Chilean ambassador to the United States under the ousted government of Salvador Allende, lived in exile in Washington, D.C., where he and others sought to influence opinion against the Pinochet dictatorship.

On September 21, 1976, Letelier and an American associate, Ronni Moffitt, were killed when their car was exploded in the heart of Washington. A U.S. judge charged the Chilean secret police with having masterminded this gangster-style crime and three of their members were indicted. The United States threatened strong measures if the Chilean agents were not extradited and brought to trial. They were not extradited. They were tried in Chile—and acquitted.

A 1980 article by Charles A. Krause in *The Washington Post* reported from Santiago, Chile, that "U.S. diplomats here now say the administration was never prepared to carry out its threats" of harsh reprisals against the Pinochet government. The Krause article continued: " 'All right, we bluffed,' said one high-ranking U.S. official here last week. 'They called our bluff and we lost.' " Krause went on to report that facing down the

"You Fellows Think I Should Have Sent A Floral Piece?"
9/28/76

"If Our Agents Are Responsible For Blowing Up People In The Capital Of The United States, That's Strictly A Chilean Internal Matter"
5/17/79

Firm Hand At The Wheel
9/20/79

United States actually bolstered and strengthened the Pinochet military regime.

We do not have to believe in old-fashioned gunboat diplomacy to find it intolerable that a gangster-type government in Chile should be able to blow up opponents in the capital of the United States without a reaction stronger than pro forma threats.

When we tell Russians or Cubans or Iranians or anyone else that something is "unacceptable," we should mean it. If we don't mean it, we shouldn't say it.

A bottom line that keeps dropping lower and lower takes our government's credibility down with it.

A policy of bluff-and-back-down is not only humiliating—it is dangerous. What happens when we really mean business and our adversaries don't believe us? ∎

"At Times Like This, The Nation Must Speak With A Single Voice"
2/7/80

The Other Aggression
1/24/80

**"Exactly! You Shouldn't Get Mixed Up
With Politics"**
1/10/80

Choice Of Torches
1/18/80

"To Each His Own Event"
5/16/80

5/28/80

"Why Aren't Our Allies Following Us?"
5/21/80

5/27/80

"Good Luck, Comrades"
3/1/78

Bay Of People
5/7/80

IT TAKES ALL KINDS

FROM TIME TO TIME we pick up a few precious pieces of wisdom that are to be treasured. For example, Chuck Jones, the genius of animated cartoons, passed along to me a Great Truth that his father had discovered: nothing looks more like a bottle than a bottle in a paper bag.

As Jones says, even before you grasp the bag, it somehow manages to fold itself around. It says "bottle!"

All wrappings don't do that so easily. A cartoonist tries to observe the politician wrapped inside the flag, the person within the pious political phrases.

Bert Lance, a Georgia banker, came to Washington as Carter's director of management and budget. His banking operations were swathed in so

4/20/75

**"Back To Wrestling With The
Great Issues"**
9/5/79

High-Wire Act
8/1/79

1/21/76

6/29/79

**"And In Next Year's Campaign, You
Promise To Clean Up The Mess In
Washington"**
7/22/79

8/24/77

9/21/77

9/18/77

**"Imagine Those Damn Newspapers Printing
These Things Put Out By Government
Agencies!"**
4/28/78

many reports and financial statements that the figure—or figures—within seemed as difficult to penetrate as the wrappings of a mummy. But there was a definite character in there.

The comptroller of the currency, in a report on Lance's banking operations, unwrapped some irregularities. But when Lance and Carter appeared before the TV cameras, they gave the impression that the comptroller had just given Lance the Seal of Good Bankkeeping Approval. Carter said, "Bert, I'm proud of you."

Some of Lance's banking affairs unwound when he came to explain them before the Senate Banking Committee in September, 1977. Lance himself appeared as a down-home country-boy banker who only tried to help out folks by "liberal overdraft policies" for use in "attracting and retaining customers." As one of the senators observed, those customers Lance was attracting and retaining included Lance himself and members of Lance's family, whose overdrafts ran into hundreds of thousands of dollars. And Lance couldn't for the life of him understand how someone could think there was anything wrong with his putting up the same collateral with two different banks—without either of them knowing he was doing this.

Lance did verbal loops and rolls in telling about a plane he purchased, sold to his bank at a higher price and continued to use largely on per-

12/23/77

4/13/78

257

sonal matters at bank expense. A second and more expensive plane purchased by the bank and used by Lance took finances still higher into the blue yonder. In a long statement reminiscent of Richard M. Checkers, Lance told of how he started as a bank clerk supporting a wife on $90 a week. Who would be crude enough to mention that she happened to be the bank president's daughter? He was a defender of the American Way. He asserted that his "human rights" were violated. He was for the Bible, and ended up quoting Abraham Lincoln. If he forgot to mention motherhood, it was only because he and his lawyer were too overcome with emotion. The whole performance was enough to make a banker weep— unless the banker happened to be one of those fellows who operated in a less "liberal" manner than Lance.

In April, 1978, the Securities and Exchange Commission and the Comptroller of the Currency brought suit against Lance, charging him with "fraud" and "deceit" and violations of federal banking and securities laws. Lance signed a consent decree in which he agreed to correct his banking practices but without confirming or denying the charges. Lance promised not to re-enter banking without first notifying federal officials so that they could determine his fitness to operate in that field.

In addition to these civil suits, Lance was later indicted and tried in Atlanta, Georgia on criminal charges. In April, 1980, he was acquitted on nine of twelve charges, with the jurors unable to reach agreement on the remaining three. Two of these counts were for filing false financial statements with a bank to get a loan, and the other was for misapplication of bank funds. These charges were later dropped.

Another character who had his day in court, although a most peculiar one, was Texan John Connally, who had been secretary of the treasury in the Nixon administration. He was tried on a bribery charge relating to events during that period. His accuser had pleaded guilty to bribery, but Connally was acquitted.

The manner in which this case was conducted was described by Fred Graham (of CBS News) in a *New Republic* article aptly titled "The Secret Trial of John Connally." The jurors were not provided with a transcript of a Nixon–Connally tape, and at the close of the Connally trial, the judge dismissed the jury without even disclosing their names.

The judge in this trial was George L. Hart, Jr. He had also been the judge when former Nixon Attorney General Richard Kleindienst pleaded guilty to "refusing to testify accurately" during his Senate confirmation hearings. Judge Hart placed him on one month's unsupervised probation and declared Kleindienst to be a man "universally respected and admired," whose crime was simply having "a heart too loyal and considerate of others."

In the Connally case Judge Hart made an early ruling that the charges in the indictment against Connally, which involved bribery, perjury, and conspiracy, be split into separate trials. He decided that the bribery trial should come first. Connally was acquitted in this trial. The cases of perjury and conspiracy were then dropped.

Connally, who had appeared before the Senate Watergate Committee and before a federal grand jury, admitted that his sworn testimony before these bodies contained many errors.

But Connally explained these easily. He said he misunderstood some of the questions. He said his memory was faulty. And he said he didn't pay much attention to the questioning by the Senate Watergate Com-

"They All Run Together"
1/26/79

mittee and the federal grand jury because he didn't think the whole thing was going to amount to "a hill of beans."

Who would attach much importance to appearances before a grand jury or a Senate committee? Not John Connally, who felt that all the Nixon tapes should have been burned on the White House lawn.

Wilson Mizner, adventurer, colorful character, and confirmed late sleeper, once received a summons to appear in court at 9:00 A.M. On the morning he was due in court, his lawyer came over, woke him, and accompanied him to make sure he would get there on time. As Mizner saw the streets filled with men and women at that hour he said, "Jeez! All these people are going to testify against me?"

All the people in these cartoons have not been in courts. All the characters here aren't even people. And there is recognition of a few good and great ones.

It takes all kinds, and here's an assorted group—with and without wrappings. ∎

"He Is The Very Model Of A Modern
NATO General"
10/3/74

"I Was Mistaken—It Is A Cherry Tree,
But I Knew Nothing About It Being There,
And I Resent This Questioning"
2/17/80

**The Brezhnev Prize
For Independent Thinking**
11/18/75

**"We've Got All The Time In The World—
However Much Time The World Still Has"**
3/2/71

Jubilee
6/7/77

**"On The Other Hand, Old Chap, She Is
A Conservative"**
5/6/79
—On Margaret Thatcher's becoming
Prime Minister

261

"Just One Little Old Loophole"
6/22/76

Off-Broadway Note
6/13/76

"Marchons! Marchons! . . ."
11/6/77

Mission Impossible
4/30/80

American Mountain
11/14/75

"I Am Optimistic That If We Give It Our Best Shot,
We Will Come Close To Achieving The Goals
Set For Us 200 Years Ago."
—*Sen. Philip Hart*
12/28/76

Friend
11/21/79

1/17/78

INCOME AND OUTGO

"THE BUSINESS OF AMERICA," said Calvin Coolidge, "is business." This view may not be as quaint as we used to think. It has become a cliché among those who oppose government spending projects to say that we can't solve problems by throwing money at them—but this generally refers to *people* problems. Business problems we throw money at. Sometimes we can even throw money at businesses that have no problems.

Broadcast commercials appear to be telling us something about business-and-people relationships. More of these commercials keep showing customers smiling at brokers, service station employees, supermart attendants, and manufacturers. "Thank you, Paine Webfoot," they say. "Thank you, Del Batteryman." "Thank you, Sunboom Electric." "Thank you, Safeshop." "Thank you, Mr. Rightwrench." Thank you, thank you, thank you.

If a Joe Public character were ridden down and clubbed by a horseman carrying a banner that said "Genghis Khan, Your Area Barbarian," he'd smile through the hoofmarks on his face and say, "Thank you, Genghis Khan."

I don't mean that all these advertisers are so bad. But the message that keeps coming through is that they shouldn't thank us for our patronage; we should thank *them*—that we kind of *owe* them something. The government seems to have this idea too.

When a big company is mismanaged and not doing so well, it lets the government know that unless Uncle Sam comes through with a lot of money, the company might just fold up. Does the government say, as it would to you or me, "Tough. Make sure your taxes are paid up before you go down the tube." No. It says, "Thank you, Chrysler Corporation. What can we do for you? You say you'd like to borrow a billion dollars? If it's okay with you, let's make it a billion and a half, just to show that we're really appreciative."

Of course, it's not quite that simple. The big company first tells the politicians that if it goes under, a lot of people are going to be thrown out of work in an election year, and there are a lot of automobile workers and several electoral votes in Michigan, bub.

The government then feels that it's helping *people*—the employees

"You Don't Understand, Gus—To Get Government Help, You Have To Goof Up On A Grand Scale"
8/24/79

Bailout
12/7/79

who would otherwise have to work under the new ownership that would probably take over the failing company. And we're helping to foster *competition* and private enterprise—although it's not explained how competition and private enterprise are fostered by giving government financing to companies that can't hack it. If the money gets paid, thanks again, and if not, thanks for the memories.

Military spending is sometimes conducted on a similar basis. The government saved Lockheed. And Lockheed was able to repay the government mostly because the government bought Lockheed products.

Military purchases, military bases, manpower, and naval construction all come under the heading of defense, but politicians often base policies on the defense of businesses—and political influence.

Some "defense spending" actually lessens national security. George C. Wilson wrote in *The Washington Post* about several costly arms programs rushed through the House of Representatives in May, 1980. These included a bill to convert A10 anti-tank warplanes to two-seaters, at an increased cost of more than a million dollars per plane. This would add an extra 1200 pounds to each plane, reducing the performance of a craft already unable to carry a full load of weaponry. The change might cost lives, planes and battles, as well as money. But it would provide extra

"You Have Just Said The Magic Word, And
Here's Another Umpty Billion Dollars"
10/6/76

"This Is The Multiple Appropriation
Retention Vehicle. It's To Hold Extra
Congressional Funds Till We Figure Out
How To Spend Them"
8/19/79

"Hey—Here's Some That Are Actually
Needed For Defense!"
1/27/77

"What Do You Mean They Don't Work
Right? They Get Rid Of The Money,
Don't They?"
11/24/76

jobs and votes in the congressional district where the plane was made. This measure sailed through the House without even a record vote.

Increased dollars in the arms budget will result in increased orders somewhere, but they don't always increase the odds on an adequate defense. Gold-plated items that run into many millions or even a billion apiece may not be just what we need.

During the Persian Gulf crises of early 1980, when our leaders spoke stirring words about defending our vital interests, the logistical maps showed, in effect, that "you can't get there from here." Whatever conventional strategy might or might not be advisable, you couldn't help but wonder whether the American giant was missile-bound, and whether we had been acquiring the right ships, planes, landing craft, and bases. Perhaps we should have looked more closely at the globe instead of at military wish books and budget books. Across-the-board budget boosts don't necessarily provide an across-the-world reach.

In civilian operations, the government sometimes gets into business partway, through corporations like Amtrak and the Postal Service. The latter is no longer under a cabinet officer; in 1973 it was set up as a quasi-public corporation to be run like a business. Ha!

One of the big accomplishments of this postal business was the

"We Always Put The Guns In Place First"
8/27/78

"Life Is Unfair, Kid"
3/16/78

"It's Only A Billion-Dollar Loss. You Can Make That Up Easily"
6/27/78

"It's A Roll Of Stamps That Won't Get Out Of Date Before It's Used Up"
5/17/78

"Now Then—Here's Our Latest List Of Absolutely Indispensable Arms Programs"
12/12/75

"What Do You Mean, It Can't Carry A Load?"
12/24/75

setting up of a package-sorting center, with a billion dollars of equipment. The packages had to be sent from other areas to this center, where the billion-dollar machinery didn't work. This system managed not only to delay but to destroy a lot of packages. You don't find many businesses that can invest a billion in an operation like that.

This hybrid organization has combined some of the worst features of government bureaucracy with some of the worst features of private monopoly.

"Junk mail," sent out by firms with impersonal mailing lists, goes at a lower rate than first-class letters. This, according to the Postal "Service," is because the firms that send out that mail bundle it and sort it.

The fact that we can individually have our names stricken from such mailing lists, if we want to, misses the point.

The trouble with junk mail is not the difficulty of tossing it into the wastebasket unopened. What's wrong is that it clogs the mails and actually delays the full-cost first-class mail. While you are waiting for some important personal or business letters, you not only get more junk mail—you probably get it earlier than the important mail because it's processed quicker.

I don't object to junk-mail firms and mailing-list houses sending out all

The Extra Load
6/11/74

"On Some Things We Can Really Move"
5/6/80

"It's One Of Ours"
3/3/77

"We Hate To Put You Out Of Your House, But We've Just Sold It To A Family For A Fantastic Price"
8/22/79

Canceling Machine
4/13/76

"And Then You Get Up On This Stand"
4/5/79

the "occupant" or "personalized" non-personal letters they want, as long as they pay the full letter rate.

The Postal "Service" increased first-class rates by 250 percent in ten years. In 1980, the Postal "Service" asked for a record 33⅓ percent increase in its first-class postage. Of course it continued to get government subsidies besides. Its income keeps going up, but the outgo of deliveries seems to keep getting slower.

Thank you, U.S. Postal "Service."

The postal problems are not the largest of the taxpayer's financial worries. His outgo for federal, state, and local taxes keeps going up, while

**"We Had To Break The Piggy Bank To Do It,
But We Finally Got The Old House Fixed Up"**
5/24/78

**"These Things Are Absolutely Necessary
To Conduct Business—Unless We Have
To Pay For Them"**
4/19/78

**"Agent Smith, Here, Will Give Us A
Report On The Three-Martini Lunch
Situation, As Soon As He Figures
Out His Notes"**
11/11/77

**"A Funny Thing Happened—Gribbet
Gribbet—On The Way Through
The Forest"**
7/21/76

**"On To The Revival Meeting—Now
Where Did We Leave That Little
Old Drum?"**
11/16/75

government promises of tax reform generally keep going down the chute. What has finally got to him is the combination of increases in every area. The success of the tax-cutting Proposition 13 in California should not have come as a great surprise—especially in a state where property taxes kept increasing while a state surplus kept increasing too.

Home-owners are troubled by the fact that when they finally get to that happy day when they can burn the mortgage, the tax bills keep rolling in —and higher than ever. A modest enough reform that could be used more widely is a downward sliding scale on property taxes after the same persons have lived in the same house during many of their working years. A forward-looking society might even bring itself to avoid penalizing home-owners for spending their money, time, and effort to improve their property.

If you build a better house, tax assessors will beat a path to your door.

In *The King and I*, the king found that western ways contained many "puzzlements." It's lucky Anna didn't need to explain to him our various tax systems.

One of the most talked-about tax reform proposals was to eliminate deductions for the one, two, three, or no-martini lunches—symbolic of many entertainment expenses. The theory for retaining these tax breaks is that such expenditures help to *make* money—the basis for deductions.

"Look—Clean, Clean Hands"
12/7/75

"We'd Be Perfectly Willing To Use Some Of Our Extra Profits To Explore Ways Of Making More Extra Profits"
4/25/79

"It Helps The Balance Of Payments"
2/24/76

"Weaponry Inflation"
8/31/79

"Well, They Told Us They'd Do More Drilling After Prices Went Up"
10/23/79

"Help! Let Go Of That Tentacle"
5/29/74

If these expenses make money, why do they need to be deducted? The guy who improves his house for his own use not only doesn't get a deduction, he pays more taxes.

The windfall profits tax for oil companies gets into income-and-outgo on a very high level. It deals with very big companies that make very big profits, and so we thank them very much.

When the price of oil keeps going up, the oil companies keep doing better. When prices are deregulated, oil companies do still better. And as world prices continue to rise, the sky is the limit. So we wonder if the companies would mind paying, in extra taxes, some portion of all the extra money they make through no effort at all. While they talk about how they are developing energy, they are buying department stores and things of that sort, and we hate to bother them when they're so busy. They don't care to share too much of the extra money they get through price deregulation, so Congress knocks down the tax on their windfall gains to a point the oil companies find endurable.

Thank you, major oil companies!

Thank you, independent oil companies (which make only $10 million a year apiece or even less)!

Meanwhile, back at the paycheck—the small taxpayer finds the deduc-

"I Didn't Realize This Thing Needed So Much Support"
11/25/77

"It All Averages Out"
10/18/78

275

"We're All In The Same Boat"
4/11/73

tions and taxes keep increasing. Some experts argue that it would be a mistake to apply some of the windfall tax money or a gasoline tax to reducing Social Security taxes. Their reasoning is that the taxpayer should know what Social Security is costing him. He knows, and it doesn't help a bit. He just wishes he knew where all his non-earmarked taxes were going. And if he gets sick without sufficient medical coverage, he wishes he knew where the money for the hospital bills is coming from.

More government expenditures for health care would cost money. But private spending for health care costs money too and sometimes wipes out private savings. Either way, it's part of the total national outgo for medical costs.

Public health also figures in the government's balancing of non-budget policies. When it relaxes anti-pollution standards, it considers this a trade-off for speeding energy production. But how about the energy of persons whose health is endangered? How does the value of people's health compare with the income and outgo of companies that are allowed to save on anti-pollution devices? The income of clean air and water is not something to be traded off for a few extra bucks or ohms or kilowatts. Nor are the homes, the lands, the forests, and other resources that would be traded off in Faustian quick deals for some temporary extra energy here or there. An Energy Mobilization Board empowered to override

Rip-Off
6/1/75

" 'I Was Thinking,' Alice Said . . . 'Which
Is The Best Way Out . . . It's Getting So
Dark . . .' But The Fat Little Men Only
Looked At Each Other And Grinned"
6/9/77

health, safety, and environmental rules might cut through red tape. But it could also cut up these protective regulations and cut up the land itself.

Some of these energy quick-fix policies recall the old Marx Brothers film, in which they chopped up all the coaches on an old railroad train to keep feeding the locomotive. This is okay for a short-term race, but a hell of a way to run a railroad.

Among the bad deals in trade-offs has been the endangering of coastal waters by leasing rights for oil exploration. And one of the worst was the leasing of the Georges Bank waters off the coast of Massachusetts.

Georges Bank is one of the great fishing areas not only of the United States but of the world. These waters produce 15 percent of the entire commercial fish catch on the planet. All of this, as well as the livelihoods and the villages of New Englanders in the area, was put on the line in the hope of finding a relatively small amount of oil.

"Then He Took The Loaves And The Fishes And
Instead Of Feeding The Multitude, He Swapped Them
For A Can Of Oil"
11/2/79

The Carter administration explained that funds would be provided for clean-ups in case of oil damage. It did not explain how it could compensate for the devastating loss of breeding areas for the fish.

Secretary of the Interior Cecil B. Andrus defended the plan in a published letter in 1979. He stated that to say the oil would only be enough to supply the country's needs for eight days at current consumption rates was like saying that all the Georges Bank fish would only provide each American with four meals of protein. He thus missed the whole point.

The prospective oil (if discovered) would be pumped out and gone. The fish, one of the greatest sources of protein on the earth, make up a constantly replenishable treasure. To destroy even part of this great resource makes the game not worth the brief energy candle involved.

Such trade-offs are bad bargains and show poor understanding of the country's income and outgo in real wealth. For such governmental bookkeeping and trading, the timber miners, the strip miners, the polluting industries, the oil companies could come out fine.

The rest of us could say, Thank you, oil and mining companies!

Thank you, Secretary of the Interior!

Thank you, Mr. President! ■

12/16/79

Break-In
12/19/79

"This Way We Only Lose The Coastline, The Fishing Industry,
The Ocean Floor, The Birds, Marine Life . . ."
12/26/76